鳥 山 明

As many of you can probably imagine, doing a weekly manga serial is very hard work. I've been doing a weekly serial for 13 years straight and it's beginning to wear me down physically and mentally. I never considered myself to be the kind of guy who had a lot of grit and willpower. So, thinking of myself and my family, I'm starting to think of ways to take it easy.

–Akira Toriyama, 1992

Widely known all over the world for his playful, innovative storytelling and humorous, distinctive art style, **Dragon Ball** creator Akira Toriyama is also known in his native Japan for the wildly popular **Dr. Slump**, his previous manga series about the adventures of a mad scientist and his android "daughter." His hit series **Dragon Ball** ran from 1984 to 1995 in Shueisha's **Weekly Shonen Jump** magazine. He is also known for his design work on video games such as **Dragon Warrior**, **Chrono Trigger** and **Tobal No. 1**. His recent manga works include **Cowa!**, **Kajika**, **Sand Land**, **Neko Majin**, and a children's book, **Toccio the Angel**. He lives with his family in Japan.

DRAGON BALL Z VOL. 17
The SHONEN JUMP Manga Edition

This graphic novel contains material that was originally published in English in **SHONEN JUMP** #19-21.

STORY AND ART BY
AKIRA TORIYAMA

English Adaptation/Gerard Jones
Translation/Lillian Olsen
Touch-up Art & Lettering/Wayne Truman
Design/Sean Lee
Editor/Jason Thompson

Editor in Chief, Books/Alvin Lu
Editor in Chief, Magazines/Marc Weidenbaum
VP of Publishing Licensing/Rika Inouye
VP of Sales/Gonzalo Ferreyra
Sr. VP of Marketing/Liza Coppola
Publisher/Hyoe Narita

In the original Japanese edition, DRAGON BALL and DRAGON BALL Z are known collectively as the 42-volume series DRAGON BALL. The English DRAGON BALL Z was originally volumes 17-42 of the Japanese DRAGON BALL.

 A CIP catalogue record for this book is available from the British Library.

Printed in the U.S.A.

Published by VIZ Media, LLC
P.O. Box 77010
San Francisco, CA 94107

SHONEN JUMP Manga Edition
10 9 8 7 6 5 4
First printing, September 2004
Fourth printing, March 2008

viz
media
www.viz.com

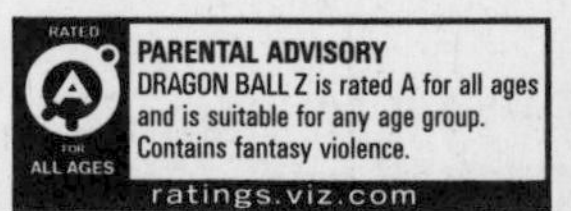
RATED
A
FOR ALL AGES
PARENTAL ADVISORY
DRAGON BALL Z is rated A for all ages and is suitable for any age group. Contains fantasy violence.
ratings.viz.com

THE WORLD'S MOST POPULAR MANGA
SHONEN JUMP
www.shonenjump.com

SHONEN JUMP MANGA

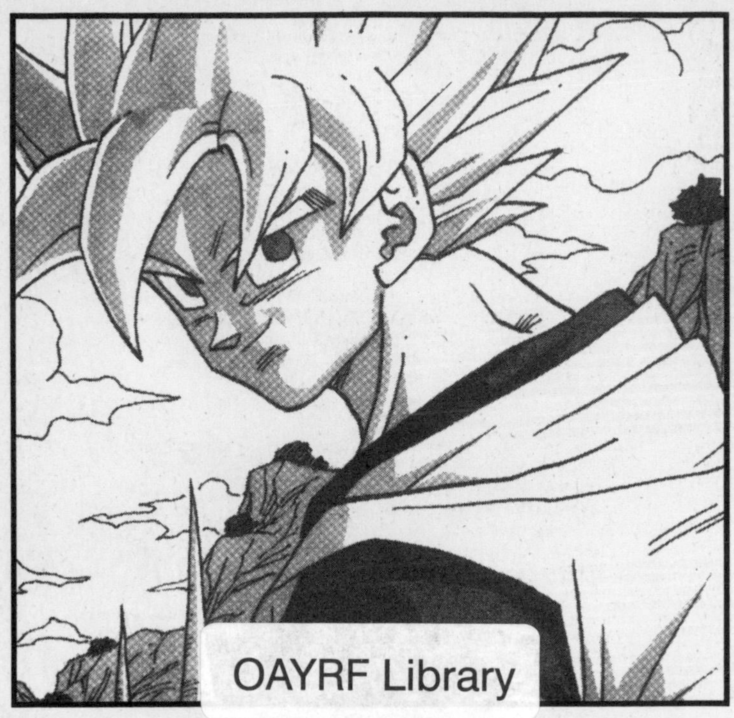

DRAGON BALL Z

Vol. 17

DB: 33 of 42

STORY AND ART BY
AKIRA TORIYAMA

THE MAIN CHARACTERS

Bulma
Goku's oldest friend, Bulma is a scientific genius.
Son Goku
The greatest martial artist on Earth, he is one of the last of the Saiyans, an almost extinct alien race. Like Trunks and Vegeta, he can power-up by transforming into a "Super Saiyan." He also has the power to teleport.
Son Gohan
Goku's young son, a half-human, half-Saiyan. Currently training with his father in the Room of Spirit and Time.
Kuririn
Goku's former martial arts schoolmate.

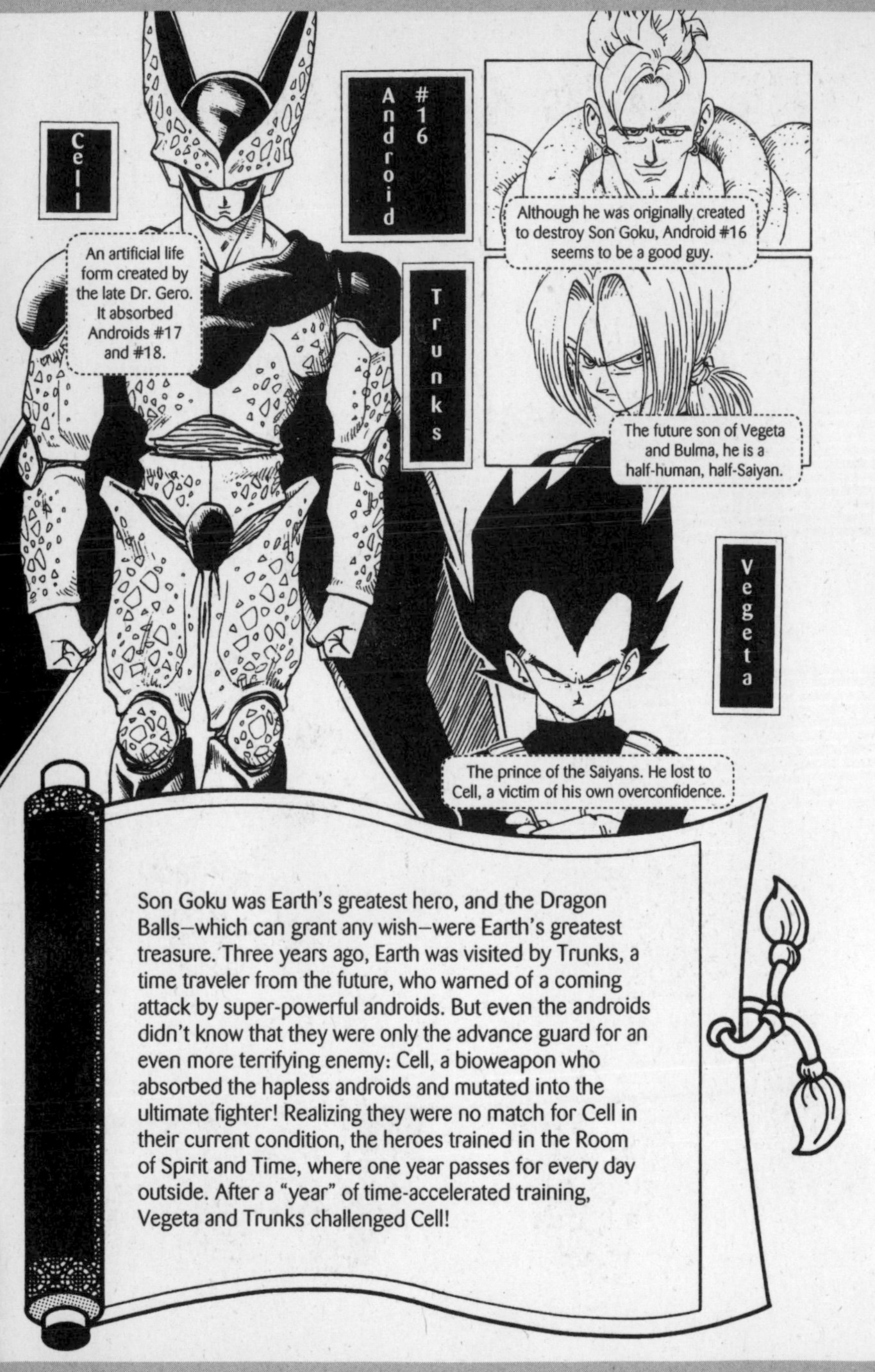
Android #16
Although he was originally created to destroy Son Goku, Android #16 seems to be a good guy.
Cell
An artificial life form created by the late Dr. Gero. It absorbed Androids #17 and #18.
Trunks
The future son of Vegeta and Bulma, he is a half-human, half-Saiyan.
Vegeta
The prince of the Saiyans. He lost to Cell, a victim of his own overconfidence.
Son Goku was Earth's greatest hero, and the Dragon Balls—which can grant any wish—were Earth's greatest treasure. Three years ago, Earth was visited by Trunks, a time traveler from the future, who warned of a coming attack by super-powerful androids. But even the androids didn't know that they were only the advance guard for an even more terrifying enemy: Cell, a bioweapon who absorbed the hapless androids and mutated into the ultimate fighter! Realizing they were no match for Cell in their current condition, the heroes trained in the Room of Spirit and Time, where one year passes for every day outside. After a "year" of time-accelerated training, Vegeta and Trunks challenged Cell!

DRAGON BALL Z 17

IT'S DA
CONTENTS.

Tale 192 Trunks Surpasses His Father! 7
Tale 193 The Balance of Power 22
Tale 194 Cell's Idea 36
Tale 195 Message of Terror 51
Tale 196 The Emergence 66
Tale 197 The Calm Before the Storm 80
Tale 198 Cell vs. the Army 94
Tale 199 The New Kami-sama 109
Tale 200 The Cell Game Begins! 124
Tale 201 Heroes Assemble! 138
Tale 202 Hercule, Champion of the World 152
Trunks: The Story 166
Title Page Gallery 185
Previews 192

DBZ: 192
Trunks Surpasses His Father!

READ THIS WAY

...
YAAA !!

NNG... GAAAH... !!!
GGGG...
H- HEY... TRUNKS !
ARE YOU OK... ?!

KA

THIS IS THE END...
VEGETA.

READ THIS WAY
...?!
RRMMMMBLE

TRUNKS...
?!

RRRMMM...
WHAT *IS* THAT...
?!

HE HASN'T EVEN BRACED HIMSELF FOR COMBAT YET... AND HE'S POURING OUT ALL THIS *CHI*...
I'LL *NEVER* GET USED TO SAIYANS...
亀

READ
THIS
WAY

KURIRIN, HERE.
COULD YOU TAKE DAD SOMEWHERE ELSE? TO MASTER MUTEN-RÔSHI'S PLACE MAYBE? AND GIVE HIM THIS *SENZU* WHEN THE TIME IS RIGHT.

S-SURE THING...!
BUT WAIT... DO YOU HAVE ANOTHER *SENZU* FOR YOURSELF?!

DON'T WORRY ABOUT ME.
I WON'T BE NEEDING ONE.

I'M GOING TO PREVAIL.

SSS!...

HE'S NOT THE TYPE TO BOAST...
BUT HOW CAN HE BE SO CONFIDENT?

READ THIS WAY

TMP

I CAN FEEL IT...
...HE HAD THAT MUCH POWER BURIED IN HIM?!

CELL! IT'S TIME.
I'M GOING TO KILL YOU.

READ THIS WAY

ZK
ZK

HEH...

THAT'S A BOLD STATEMENT, TRUNKS.
ZK
ZK

READ THIS WAY

ZK
ZK

VNNN
FSH

READ
THIS
WAY

VIP
HWUD

READ
THIS
WAY

WOK

POW
POW
POW

POINT
POINT

OH... !
O'COURSE... HE'S LEADING CELL AWAY FROM VEGETA!!

READ THIS WAY

BOW
RRG
BM
KRAK

READ THIS WAY

BMBM

B-B-B-B-BM

Tp

WOK

READ
THIS
WAY

ZZUUZZZZZ

FSH

HMP

CAN YOU FINALLY FIGHT FREELY?
NOW THAT VEGETA'S SAFE ?

HEH..

!

I DIDN'T EXPECT YOU TO LET HIM GO.
WHY NOT? HE DOESN'T AMUSE ME ANY-MORE.

READ THIS WAY

IT'S ***YOUR*** POWERS I'M INTERESTED IN.

...

I CAN'T WAIT! IT'S TIME TO KNOW JUST HOW POWERFUL I AM—***COMPLETE***!

HWOOSH

THEN HERE COMES YOUR CHANCE!

NEXT: Advantages and Disadvantages

DBZ: 193 • The Balance of Power

HOOSH

BZZBZZ

BZZT

WHAT YOU'RE ABOUT TO SEE NOW...
...IS MY TRUE POWER !!!

READ THIS WAY

YES.
AND IT IS MAGNIF-ICENT POWER.
GREATER THAN MINE BY A WIDE MARGIN.
BUT THEN, POWER ISN'T EVERY-THING...
...I ASSURE YOU.
...?!
HMP. NICE BLUFF!

SHH

BOW!

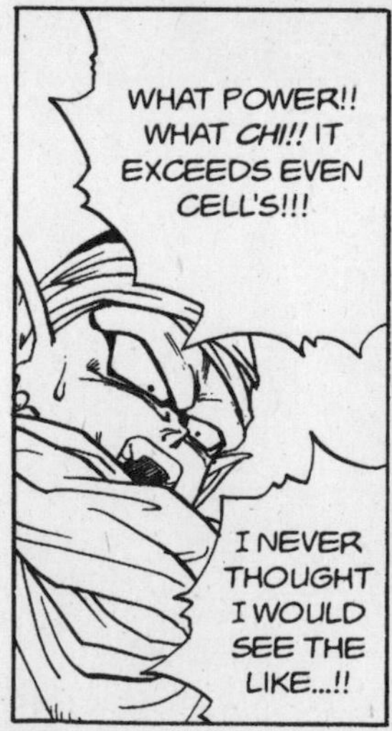
WHAT POWER!! WHAT *CHI!!* IT EXCEEDS EVEN CELL'S!!!
I NEVER THOUGHT I WOULD SEE THE LIKE...!!

READ THIS WAY

WHAT?! WHO ARE YOU TALKING ABOUT ?!
DON'T JUST WATCH!! TELL US WHAT'S GOING ON!!

I'M TALKING ABOUT **TRUNKS**, OF COURSE !!

TRUNKS ?!
MY LITTLE BOY !!!

BOOM

READ THIS WAY

BAM

VIII

VIII

SH-SHOOM

B-BAM

!

WHOA! HE'S PRO-GRESSED SO FAST...!

AT THIS RATE HE COULD REALLY TURN INTO SOME-THING !!

VIIII

READ THIS WAY

BAM

DAD'S BEEN THERE SO LONG–JUST *SITTING* THERE–
WHAT'S HE THINKING? CAN HE REALLY *SURPASS* THE STATE...

NNH !!!
UNH !!!
HWOOOO

READ THIS WAY

DMM

FSH

HFF HFF
WHEEZ

BOOOM

GGG

HUH-
HHH...

READ THIS WAY

DOM

BRR BRR
WOW !!!!

DAD !!!
YOU DID IT!!!

YOU SURPASSED THE STATE OF SUPER SAIYAN!!!

READ THIS WAY

...
...AND I CAN DO ONE MORE NOTCH!
HUH ?!

HYAAAH...!!!!
BM
HOOM
G.G.G

READ THIS WAY
BZZT
KXXK
YOU...
YOU DID IT!!!!
TH-THIS IS INCREDIBLE!!!
YOU CAN TAKE CELL EASILY NOW!!!
...

READ
THIS
WAY

DYAH
!!!

FSH

VNNn

VNN

HRRR
!!!

FSH

VNn

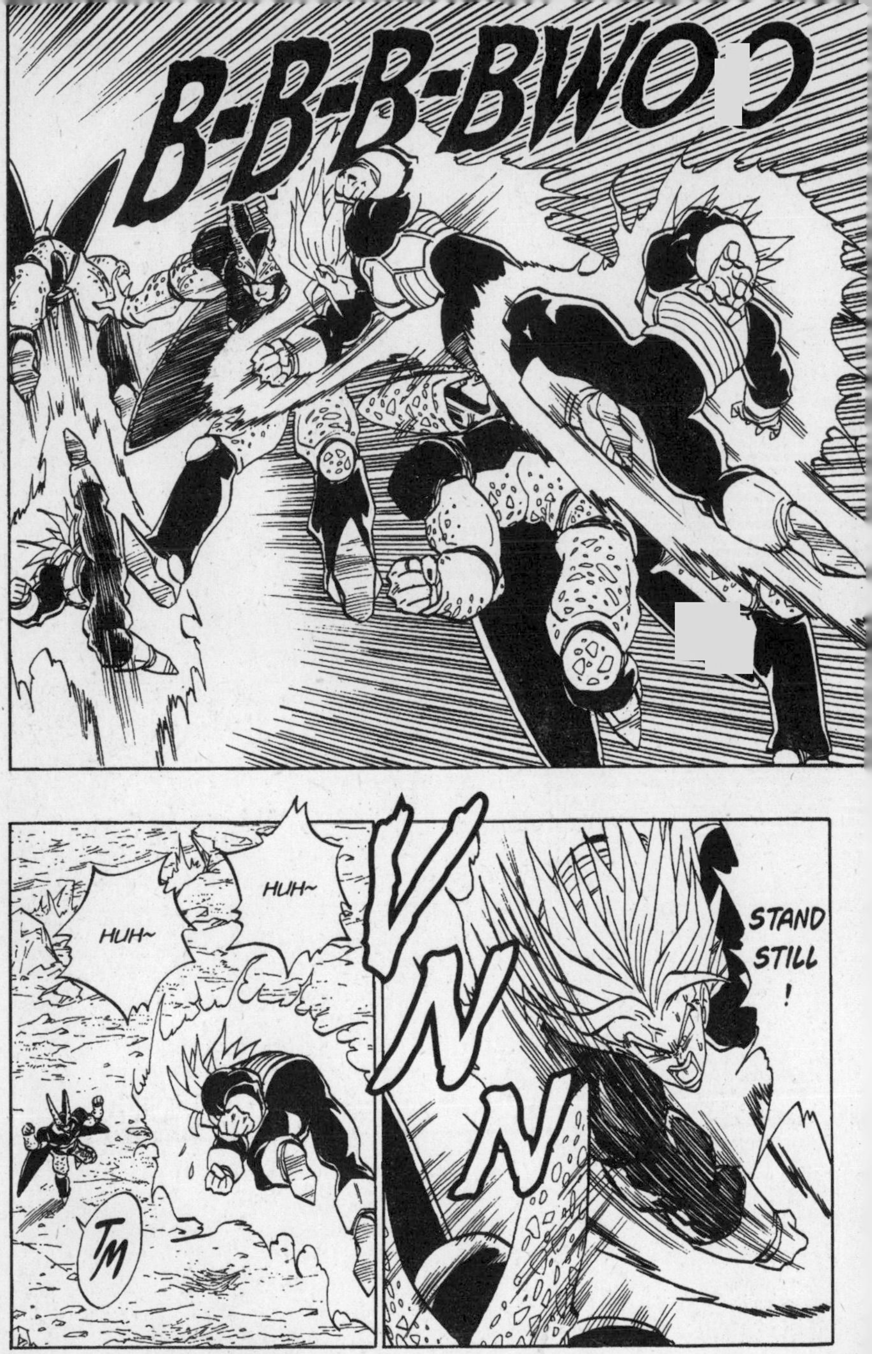

B-B-B-BWO

HUH~

HUH~

TM

VNN

STAND STILL!

READ THIS WAY

...COULD I BEAT HIM LIKE THIS...?
NO... PROBABLY NOT...

HUH ?!
ALL THIS NEW MASS GIVES ME STRENGTH, BUT IT KILLS MY SPEED.

ALL THE POWER IN THE WORLD WON'T DO ANY GOOD IF I CAN'T HIT THE GUY!
Pff

THIS CONSUMES TOO MUCH ENERGY, TOO.
ALL IN ALL—THE REGULAR SUPER SAIYAN IS BEST!
AT LEAST NOW I KNOW.

FROM NOW ON WE'LL TRY TO MAKE SUPER SAIYAN OUR NATURAL FORM—AND STAY IN IT!
WE'VE GOT TO WORK ON GETTING RID OF THAT INSTABILITY... THAT RESTLESS FEELING.

WE'VE GOTTA START OVER FROM BASIC TRAINING !
IT SEEMS LIKE THE LONG WAY—BUT IT'S THE BEST WAY TO GO.

OKAY !!

READ
THIS
WAY

IMPOSSIBLE...!!
H-HOW CAN THIS BE...?!
WHY CAN'T I *GET* HIM?!
YOU'RE STILL SO GREEN. YOU HAVEN'T FIGURED IT OUT?
YOU SAID YOU'D SHOW ME YOUR TRUE POWER, BUT HERE YOU ARE, RELYING ON BRUTE FORCE.
DOOM
SUCH A TRANSFORMATION IS NOTHING... AS YOU CAN SEE!

NEXT: The Truce

DBZ: 194 • Cell's Idea

YOU WERE A FOOL.
WHAT GOOD IS A TRANSFORMATION THAT ONLY GIVES YOU BRUTE STRENGTH?

HSS

FSS...

...

I...I WAS AN IDIOT...

...CELL IS RIGHT...

SO THAT'S WHY DAD CHOSE NOT TO TRANSFORM THIS WAY...

HE KNEW THIS WOULD HAPPEN...

READ THIS WAY

FSS

TP

...I HAVE NO CHANCE NOW...
JUST KILL ME... !

MAYBE I WILL.

READ THIS WAY

!!

T-TRUNKS'S CHI SUDDENLY SHRUNK...!!!
BUT CELL'S IS STILL HUGE!

WH-WHAT HAPPENED?!
IS IT OVER...?!

TH-THIS CAN'T BE...!!!
HE WAS SO SURE HE'D WIN...!!!
V-VEGETA!! GET UP!! EAT THIS SENZU!!

YOU AND VEGETA WERE SUCH BIG DISAPPOINTMENTS.

I THOUGHT I'D HAVE MORE FUN...

...

HEY!! HAS TRUNKS WON YET?!

THE COMPLETE CELL...

...IS BEYOND BELIEF...

...TRUNKS IS GOING TO **DIE**!!

WHAT?!

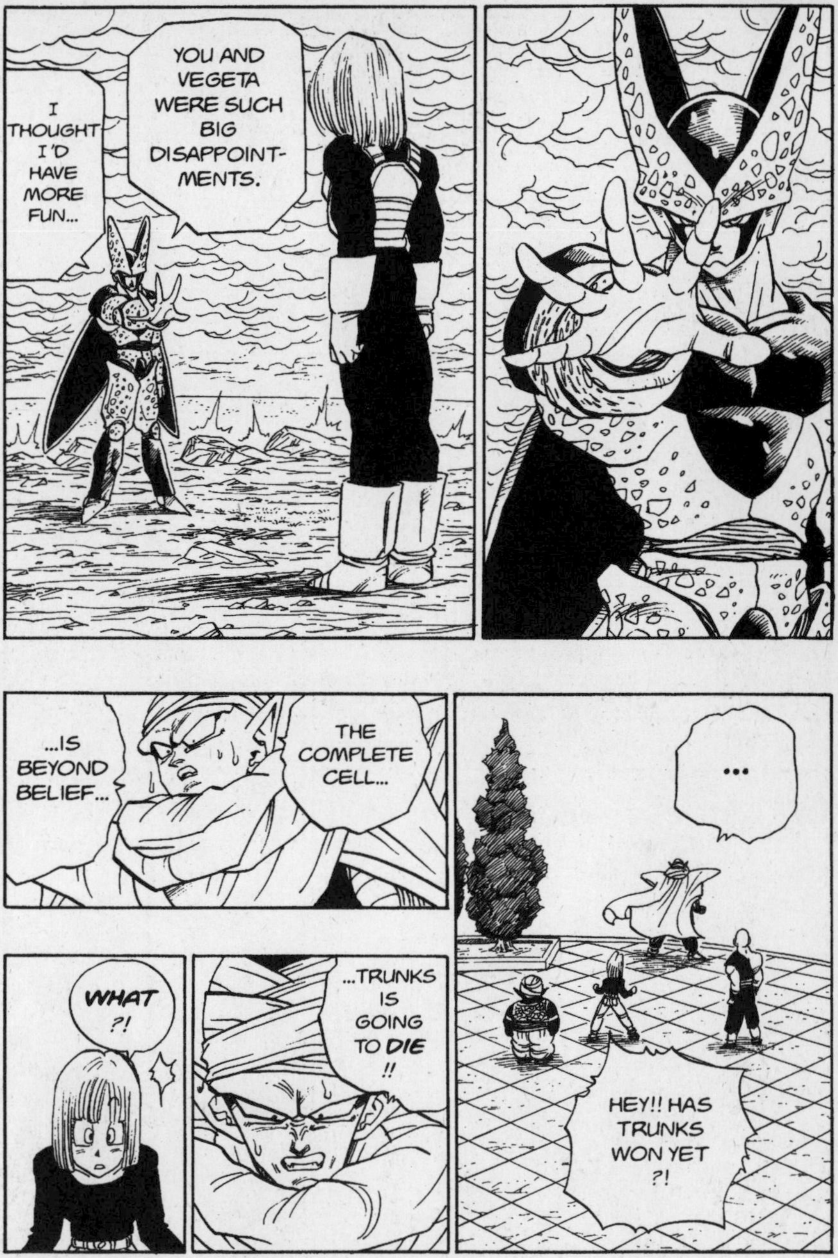

READ THIS WAY

YOU WEREN'T IN MY LEAGUE, BUT YOU AND VEGETA DID BOTH IMPROVE DRAMATICALLY IN A SHORT PERIOD OF TIME.
ONE LAST QUESTION.

HOW DID YOU DO THAT?
...
FINE. SO DON'T TELL ME. TRY THIS QUESTION INSTEAD...

WOULD YOU IMPROVE FURTHER IF YOU HAD THE TIME?
!?
WELL?
...HOW SHOULD I KNOW...?! I WON'T KNOW UNTIL I TRY!
BUT WHY ARE YOU ASKING THIS...?

READ THIS WAY

HMPH...
SO IT'S NOT IMPOS- SIBLE...

MY NEXT QUESTION IS... WHAT'S SON GOKU DOING ?
WHY HASN'T HE SHOWN UP HERE ?

...GOKU IS TRAINING TO DEFEAT YOU! YOU'LL MEET HIM SOON ENOUGH!
AND HE'LL DO WHAT I FAILED TO DO !

HEH!!
GOOD ANSWER.

READ THIS WAY

ALL RIGHT...
I'LL OPEN A TOURNAMENT.

A...
...TOURNAMENT?

10 DAYS FROM NOW.
I'M BEING GENEROUS. GET STRONGER. MAKE ME HAPPY.

WH-WHAT ARE YOU TRYING TO DO...?!
YOU MAY NOT HAVE HEARD OF IT...
...BUT THERE USED TO BE A MARTIAL ARTS TOURNAMENT CALLED "STRONGEST UNDER THE HEAVENS."
I'M GOING TO RE-CREATE IT.

BUT ALL OF YOU WILL ONLY HAVE ME TO FIGHT. WE'LL FIGHT ONE ON ONE, AND IF I WIN, WE GO TO THE NEXT ONE.
I DON'T CARE HOW MANY OF YOU THERE ARE. THE MORE THE MERRIER. SO YOU'D BETTER START GATHERING ALLIES.

READ
THIS
WAY

I'LL LET YOU KNOW THE LOCATION LATER.
KEEP WATCHING THE TV NEWS.
WH-WHAT?!

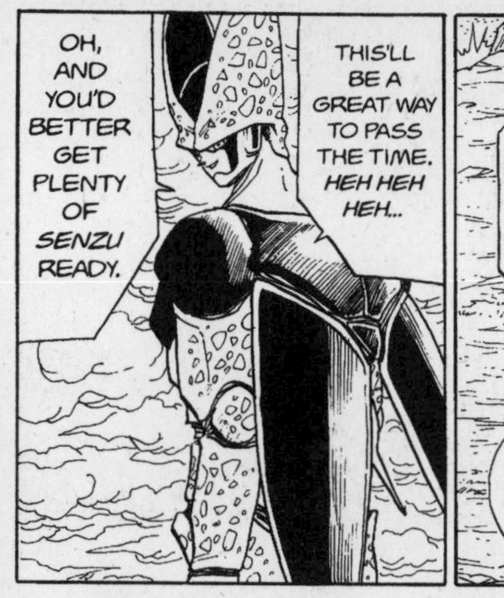
THIS'LL BE A GREAT WAY TO PASS THE TIME. HEH HEH HEH...
OH, AND YOU'D BETTER GET PLENTY OF SENZU READY.

C-CELL, WAIT...!! WHAT'S THE POINT OF THIS TOURNAMENT?! WHAT DO YOU WANT, ANYWAY...?!
I DON'T UNDERSTAND IT!! DO YOU WANT TO TAKE OVER EARTH... THE GALAXY?!

I WANT TO CONFIRM MY SUPERIORITY.... AND SPREAD SOME FEAR OVER THIS WORLD.
IT'LL BE GOOD PRACTICE, TOO.

WHAT DO I WANT? NOTHING MATERIAL.
I WAS CREATED TO KILL SON GOKU, BUT THERE'S LITTLE POINT TO THAT NOW.

READ THIS WAY

MAYBE I JUST WANT TO HAVE FUN. AND THE GREATEST FUN...
IS TO SEE PEOPLE'S FACES CONTORTED IN TERROR!

...WHAT... ?!

YEAH. JUST LIKE THAT.
HA HA HA!

PIP

BM

...

HEY !!

TH- THANK GOD!! HE'S ALIVE !!

BUT WHAT HAPPENED?! WHERE'S CELL ?!

DON'T JUST STAND THERE!! GO SAVE HIM!!

DON'T LET MY BABY DIE!!!

...DON'T WORRY... HE'S ALL RIGHT...

REALLY ?!

B...

BUT **WHY**... ?!

...

READ THIS WAY

...LOOKS LIKE I'LL HAVE TO TAKE MY TURN IN THE ROOM OF SPIRIT AND TIME...

TH-THAT'S WHAT IT SAID... ?!

A...
...A TOURNAMENT ?!

IT'S TOYING WITH US...
CURSE IT...!!

BUT WHO'D ENTER A THING LIKE THAT ?!
NOT EVEN YOU GUYS STOOD A CHANCE !!

...WHEN GOKU COMES OUT...
I'M GOING TO TRAIN ONCE MORE IN THE ROOM OF SPIRIT AND TIME.

READ THIS WAY

WE DON'T NEED YOU **OR** GOKU. I ONLY NEED THE **ROOM** FOR ONE MORE DAY.
CELL WILL REGRET GIVING ME MORE TIME...

...

...

I... I'LL DO IT...

I'LL ENTER THE TOURNAMENT...

SCFF

YOU... ?!

...PLEASE... TAKE ME TO CAPSULE CORP. SO I CAN GET REPAIRED.

...I'LL DO WHATEVER I CAN...

READ THIS WAY

DO YOU THINK WE WANT YOU ?!
ANOTHER ONE OF DR. GERO'S CREATIONS ?!

...

SURE. I'LL TAKE YOU.
KURIRIN... !!

DON'T WORRY, TRUNKS. I DON'T THINK HE'S A BAD GUY.
THE TWO THAT CELL SWALLOWED WEREN'T THAT BAD EITHER.
THEY'RE NOT EXACTLY LIKE THE ANDROIDS IN YOUR FUTURE...

...AND DON'T WE WANT AS MANY ALLIES AS WE GET CAN RIGHT NOW?
...
OOF.
THANKS...

HMPH...

THE NEXT DAY CAME THE TV BROADCAST THAT TRANSMITTED HORROR ACROSS THE GLOBE...

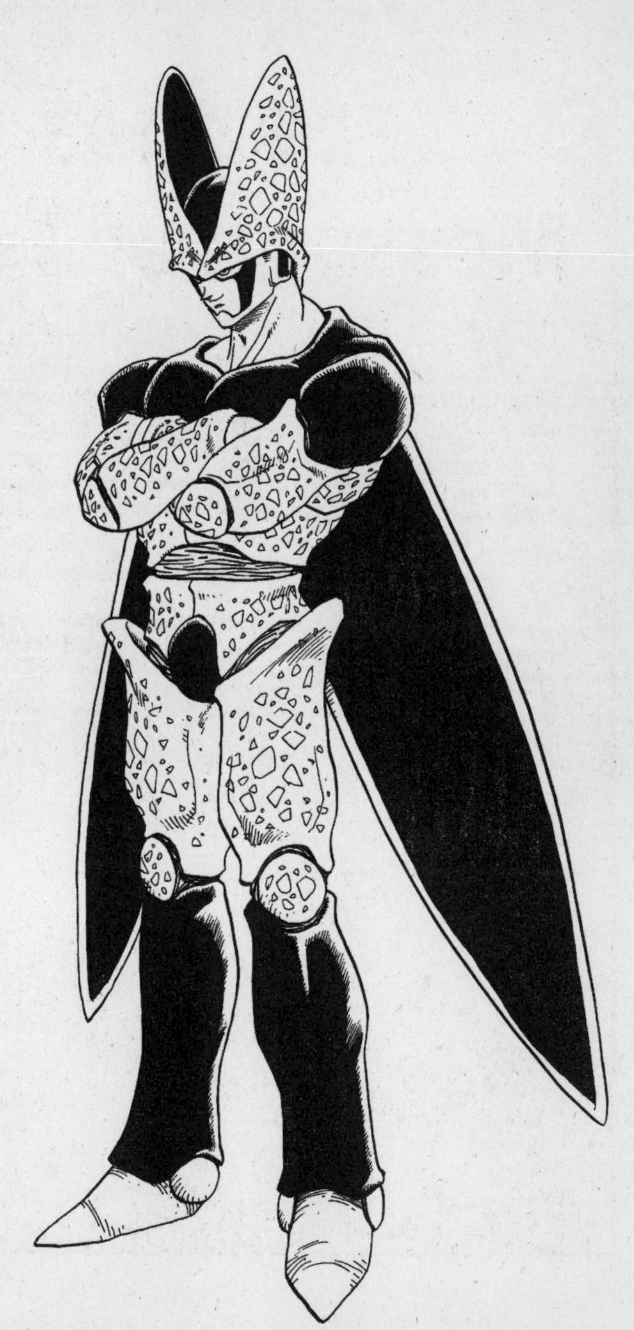

DBZ: 195
Message of Terror

THE NEXT MORNING...
WELL... THIS LOOKS LIKE A DANDY SPOT...
...FOR A BLOODY TOURNAMENT.

READ
THIS
WAY

TP

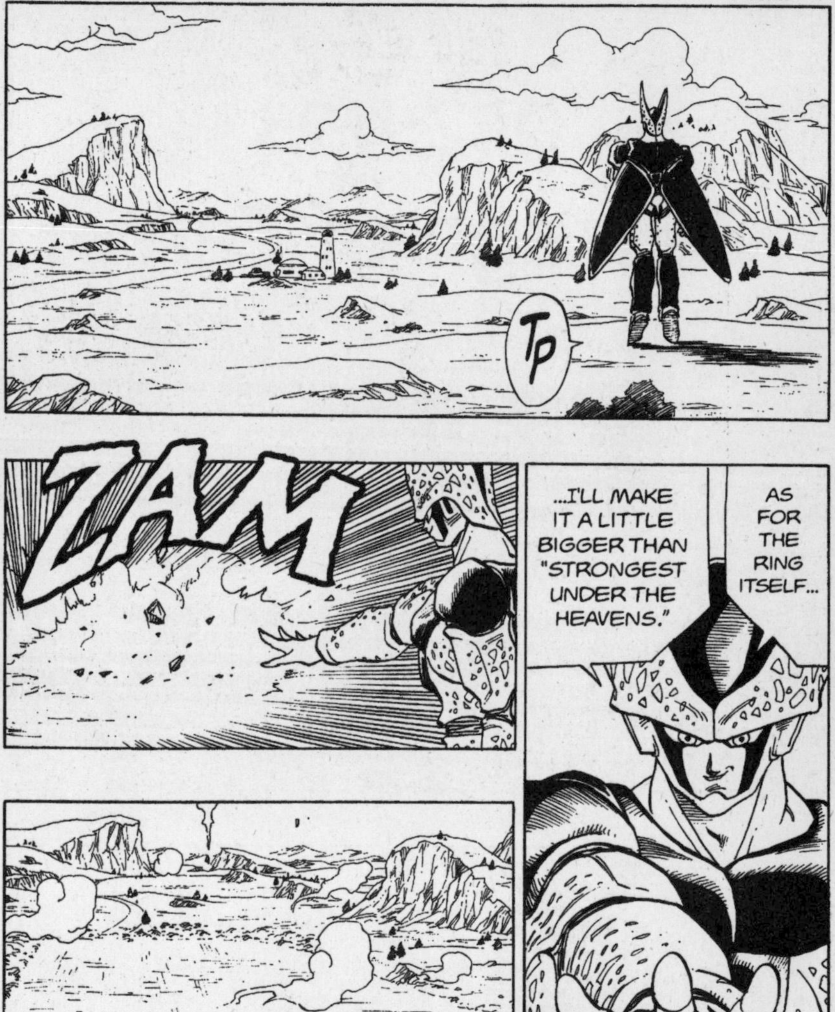

AS FOR THE RING ITSELF...

...I'LL MAKE IT A LITTLE BIGGER THAN "STRONGEST UNDER THE HEAVENS."

ZAM

READ THIS WAY

WGG

NEXT...

BIII
B-BIII

WOK

I FIGURED THERE'D BE QUALITY ROCK AROUND HERE.

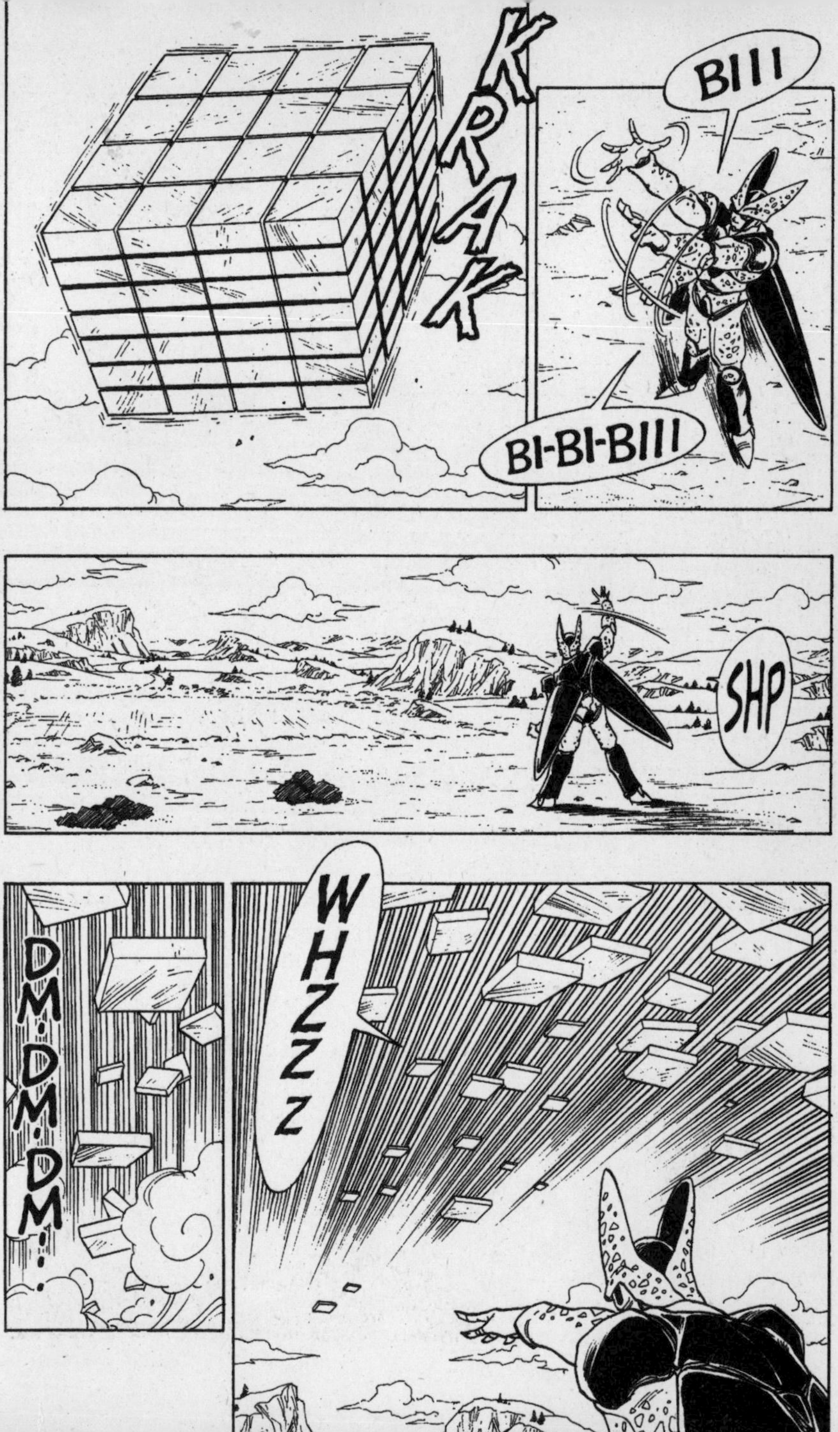

KRAK
BIII
BI-BI-BIII

SHP

DM.DM.DM...
WHZZZ

READ
THIS
WAY

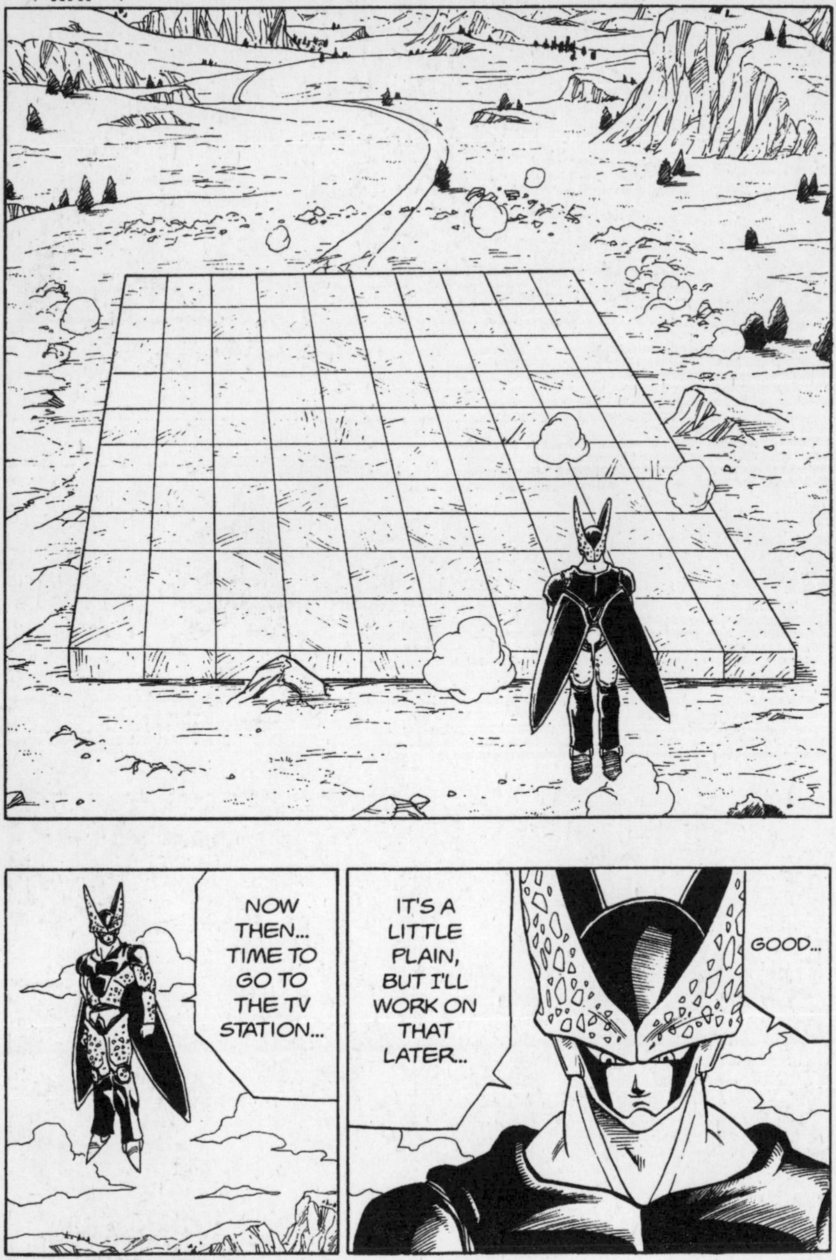

GOOD...
IT'S A LITTLE PLAIN, BUT I'LL WORK ON THAT LATER...

NOW THEN... TIME TO GO TO THE TV STATION...

READ THIS WAY

HYUUU

...AND NOW FOR THE WEATHER AROUND THE GLOBE...

H-HEY, WHO ARE YOU?! WHAT ARE YOU DOING... ?!
GAH !!!

TH-
THERE IT IS !!!

READ THIS WAY

MASTER MUTEN-RÔSHI !
IT'S CELL !!!
HE'S ON TV!!

WH-WHAT ?!
SO THAT'S CELL... ?!

C-CALL SECURITY !!
CALL THE COPS TOO, NOW !!

WAH... GAH... !!
TH-THIS IS TOO BRUTAL... !
THAT MONSTER...

GOOD MORNING, EVERYONE.
I'LL BE INTERRUPTING YOUR REGULARLY SCHEDULED PROGRAMMING FOR JUST A MOMENT...

READ THIS WAY

...TO BRING YOU SOME GREAT NEWS! I KNOW AS YOU GO THROUGH YOUR LITTLE LIVES OF PEACE AND HAPPINESS...

...THAT YOU CRAVE JUST A BIT MORE EXCITEMENT IN YOUR HUMDRUM DAYS.

STUDIO

STUDIO

WELL. MY NAME IS CELL.
I'M SURE YOU'VE ALL HEARD OF THE MONSTER WHO SLAUGHTERED SOME PEOPLE A FEW DAYS AGO.
THAT WAS ME! ONLY I'VE ADVANCED AND GROWN MORE POWERFUL SINCE.

WH... WHAT... ?!!
ZZTV
99

...THANK YOU FOR PROVIDING ME WITH SO MUCH LIFE ENERGY.
DON'T WORRY. I WON'T BE NEEDING ANY MORE...
ZZTV

READ THIS WAY

SO, AS FOR THIS WONDERFUL NEWS...
...NINE DAYS FROM NOW, ON THE 17TH, AT NOON...
BZZ
BZZ

I'M STARTING A MARTIAL ARTS TOURNAMENT, THE "CELL GAME"!
I'VE PREPARED A RING NORTHWEST OF CENTRAL CITY, AT POINT 5 OF REGION 28 KS.

UNLIKE YOUR *TENKA'ICHI BUDÔKAI*, YOU HUMANS WILL ONLY FIGHT ME. YOU CAN HAVE AS MANY ON YOUR SIDE AS YOU WANT.
YOU WILL FIGHT ME ONE BY ONE, WITH THE NEXT TAKING OVER ONCE THE FIRST HAS LOST.
EVEN I ***MIGHT*** GET TIRED AFTER MANY ROUNDS...
THUS THE GREATER NUMBER OF COMPETITORS YOU HAVE, THE BIGGER YOUR ADVANTAGE.

**TENKA'ICHI BUDÔKAI="STRONGEST UNDER THE HEAVENS" MARTIAL ARTS TOURNAMENT*

READ
THIS
WAY

THE RULES ARE MOSTLY THE SAME AS THE *TENKA'ICHI BUDŌKAI*. YOU LOSE IF YOU SURRENDER OR IF A PART OF YOUR BODY TOUCHES THE GROUND OUTSIDE THE RING.
YOU'LL ALSO LOSE IF YOU GET KILLED... THOUGH I'LL *TRY* TO GO EASY.

ARROGANT JERK—!

AND IN THE END, WHEN I'M THE VICTOR...

I WILL KILL EVERY SINGLE HUMAN BEING ON THIS PLANET.
I'LL COME METHODICALLY AFTER EVERY LAST ONE OF YOU, AND I'LL WATCH YOUR FACES TWIST WITH FEAR.

!!

READ THIS WAY
WH... WHAT... ?!

I WELCOME ANY AND ALL WHO THINK THEY'VE GOT WHAT IT TAKES TO BEAT ME!

ZP

HAH!!!
ZZZ

READ
THIS
WAY

B-B-B-B-BM
ZZT

YAAA
!
IF YOU DON'T WANT TO TURN OUT LIKE THIS—
ZZT

YOU'D BETTER FIND SOMEONE WHO CAN FIGHT.

READ THIS WAY

BM

...

WHAT...
WHAT A FIEND...

K-KILL EVERYONE ON EARTH...?
WHO COULD EVER FIGHT THAT THING...? NOT VEGETA... NOT TRUNKS... COULD GOKU, EVEN...?

IT'S HORRI-BLE...
...GOING SOME-WHERE, VEGETA? TRAINING?

WHAT ELSE? I'M GOING INSIDE THAT ROOM AGAIN.
I DON'T CARE HOW MANY EARTHLINGS DIE—BUT I CAN'T SIT STILL UNTIL I KILL THAT THING.

READ THIS WAY

I'M GOING TOO !
LET ME GIVE YOU A HAIRCUT FIRST.
THIS MUST GET IN YOUR EYES...
TH-THANKS...
HMPH..

CELL'S BROADCAST FILLED THE EARTH'S POPULATION WITH OVERWHELMING FEAR.
THE WORLD HAD NO FAITH IN THE MILITARY OR THE POLICE, MARGINALIZED AFTER YEARS OF PEACE. THE WORLD HAD NO FAITH IN ITS CHAMPIONS.

BUT THE WORLD HAD FORGOTTEN THAT LONG AGO, THERE LIVED A LITTLE BOY WHO FOUGHT THE GREAT DEMON KING PICCOLO.

READ
THIS
WAY

THE WORLD HAD FORGOTTEN THE WARRIOR WHO TURNED ASIDE THE THREAT OF THE SAIYANS AND FREEZA.

THE WORLD HAD FORGOTTEN SON GOKU.

NEXT: Goku and Gohan Emerge

CELL'S TV BROADCAST SHOCKED THE WORLD. MASS PANIC ENSUED AS PEOPLE HOARDED SUPPLIES AND SCRAMBLED TO THE REMOTEST LOCATIONS IN A FUTILE EFFORT TO MAKE THEMSELVES LESS OF A TARGET. CHAOS WAS EVERYWHERE...

DBZ: 196 • The Emergence

READ THIS WAY

HOW MUCH LONGER UNTIL GOKU AND GOHAN COME OUT...?
STILL THERE ARE NEARLY 3 HOURS TO GO.

HA. IF THEY COME OUT ON TIME.
THIS WILL TAKE THEM LONGER THAN 24 HOURS.

THERE'S NO NEED TO RUSH. WE HAVE 9 DAYS UNTIL THE TOURNAMENT.
IT HASN'T EVEN BEEN A DAY SINCE YOU TWO WERE IN THERE. YOU SHOULD REST SOME MORE... ***I'LL*** GO IN FIRST.

DON'T WASTE OUR TIME! NO ONE BUT A SAIYAN CAN DO ANY GOOD NOW!
...BUT IF IT WILL AMUSE YOU, DO IT. I'LL TAKE THE OTHER 8 DAYS FOR MYSELF.
ALWAYS THE ARROGANT FOOL, AREN'T YOU, VEGETA? NO ONE CAN SPEND MORE THAN 48 HOURS IN THE ***ROOM OF SPIRIT AND TIME***— TOTAL. LIFELONG.

READ THIS WAY

OH?! AND WHAT IF I CHOOSE TO?!
THEN THE EXIT DISAPPEARS— AND YOU STAY IN FOREVER.

FEH...

...BUT WE CAN STILL SPEND OVER 20 HOURS.

EH ?!

IT'S GOKU'S CHI !
THEY'VE COME OUT ALREADY ?!

WHAT... ?!
WHY SO SOON... ?

READ THIS WAY
HUH?! VEGETA AND TRUNKS ARE STILL HERE...
...BUT I CAN FEEL CELL'S *CHI* TOO, SO IT MUST BE ALIVE!
WHAT'S GOING ON HERE...?

READ
THIS
WAY

THIS... IS GOHAN ?!
ASTONISHING...

TELL US WHAT HAPPENED.

UH...

READ THIS WAY

...WHAT'S HAPPENED TO THEM ?!
THEY LOOK LIKE SUPER SAIYANS... BUT I DON'T FEEL THE ENERGY... !

IT'S LIKE...IT'S THEIR NATURAL STATE...

...SO THAT'S IT...

READ THIS WAY

A TOURNAMENT, HUH?
SOUNDS EXCITING...
"EXCITING"... ?
MR. POPO, DO YOU STILL HAVE MY GI?
MM. POPO KEPT IT.
I'M SURE MY MOM WILL MAKE YOU A NEW SET OF ARMOR.
THAT'S OKAY. I LIKE THIS ONE.
I WANT TO FIGHT AS AN EARTHLING.
I WANT SOME NEW CLOTHES TOO. CLOTHES JUST LIKE YOURS.
PIC-COLO ?

READ THIS WAY

HEH!
...OF COURSE. CONSIDER THEM MY GIFT TO YOU.

HA HA !!
THANKS, PICCOLO !

READ
THIS
WAY

...SO. TALK.
DO YOU THINK YOU CAN BEAT CELL?

I DUNNO. I HAVEN'T SEEN IT SINCE ITS METAMORPHOSIS.
I'LL GO CHECK IT OUT NOW.

HMM... LET'S SEE...
...

FUU

READ THIS WAY

THAT SHOULD DO FOR DECORATIONS...

SS..

READ THIS WAY

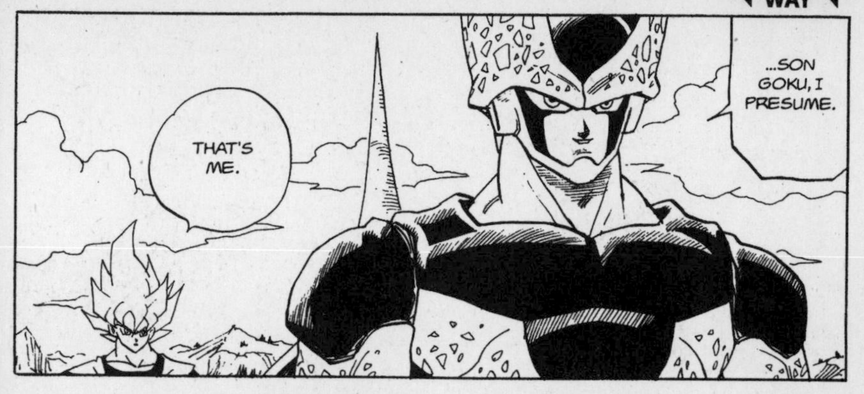
...SON GOKU, I PRESUME.
THAT'S ME.

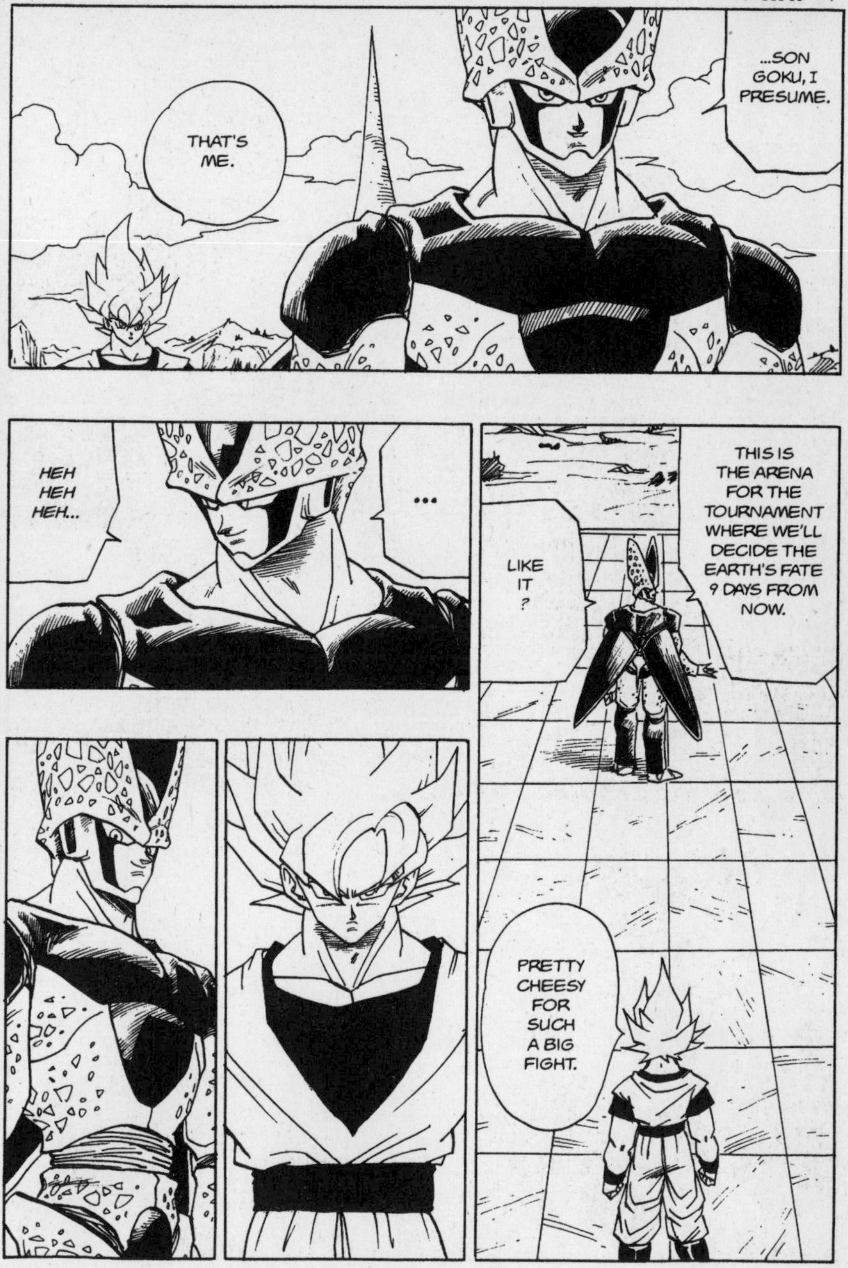

THIS IS THE ARENA FOR THE TOURNAMENT WHERE WE'LL DECIDE THE EARTH'S FATE 9 DAYS FROM NOW.

LIKE IT?

PRETTY CHEESY FOR SUCH A BIG FIGHT.

...

HEH HEH HEH...

READ THIS WAY

SO YOU DID IT.
THIS IS YOUR "COMPLETE" FORM, HUH?

...
......IT IS.

I'LL FIGHT IN YOUR TOURNAMENT...
IF YOU DON'T KILL ANYBODY ELSE UNTIL THEN. GOT IT?
HEH!

READ THIS WAY

IT'LL BE A GOOD FIGHT.

FUU

SON GOKU AT LAST...
IT LOOKS LIKE THIS WILL BE MORE FUN THAN I EXPECTED.

SS..
GOKU... WH-WHAT DID YOU THINK?!

...FRANKLY, I DIDN'T THINK IT WOULD GET THAT MUCH STRONGER.
NO WAY OF KNOWING HOW POWERFUL IT'LL BE WHEN IT FINALLY GETS DOWN TO BUSINESS.

READ THIS WAY

I WON'T REALLY KNOW UNTIL I TRY...

BUT AS I AM NOW I PROBABLY DON'T HAVE A CHANCE.

...

IT'S...

...THAT POWERFUL?

...I WAS AFRAID OF THAT...

THEN USE THE ROOM OF SPIRIT AND TIME AGAIN.

WE'VE JUST DECIDED THAT I WOULD GO FIRST, THEN VEGETA...

THEN TRUNKS... THEN YOU TWO.

I'M SORRY... I CAN'T... I'LL NEVER BE A MATCH AGAINST THAT...

NAH. GOHAN AND I WILL PASS. WE'LL TRAIN OUT HERE.

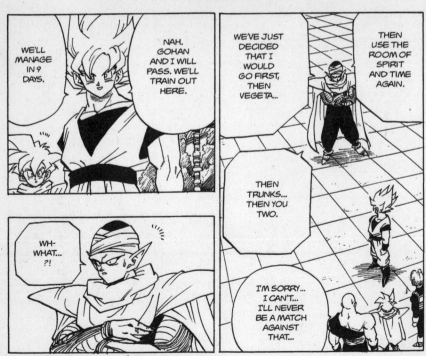

WE'LL MANAGE IN 9 DAYS.

WH-WHAT...?!

NEXT: Rest and Preparation

DBZ: 197 • The Calm Before the Storm

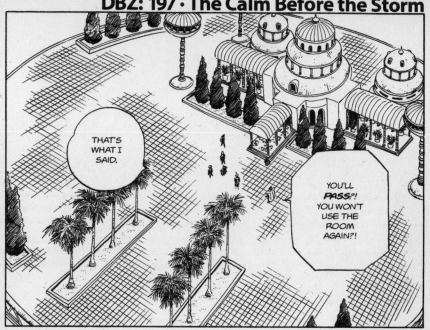

YOU'LL **PASS?!** YOU WON'T USE THE ROOM AGAIN?!
THAT'S WHAT I SAID.

WHY...? YOU STILL HAVE ANOTHER DAY BEFORE YOU'VE USED ALL YOUR TIME!

IT'S PRETTY ROUGH IN THERE, EVEN IF YOU'RE NOT DOING ANYTHING.
I'LL DO BETTER RESTING MY BODY.

HA! EVEN THE GREAT KAKARROT...
...ADMITS DEFEAT AGAINST THE RIGORS OF THE ROOM.

READ THIS WAY

MAYBE. BUT THERE'S A POINT WHERE STRESSING YOUR BODY MORE IS JUST TORTURE, NOT TRAINING.
I'VE GOT NOTHING AGAINST YOU GUYS USING THE ROOM, THOUGH. YOU'VE PROBABLY STILL GOT ROOM TO IMPROVE.

WHAT DID YOU SAY?!
ARE YOU SUGGESTING THAT ***YOU*** ARE MORE ADVANCED THAN ***I*** AM?!
UH-HUH. A LOT.

WHAT... ?!
GOOD LUCK, EVERY-BODY! WE'LL MEET AGAIN AT THE TOURNA-MENT!

READ THIS WAY

LET'S GO, GOHAN!
Y... YEAH...
BM
BM

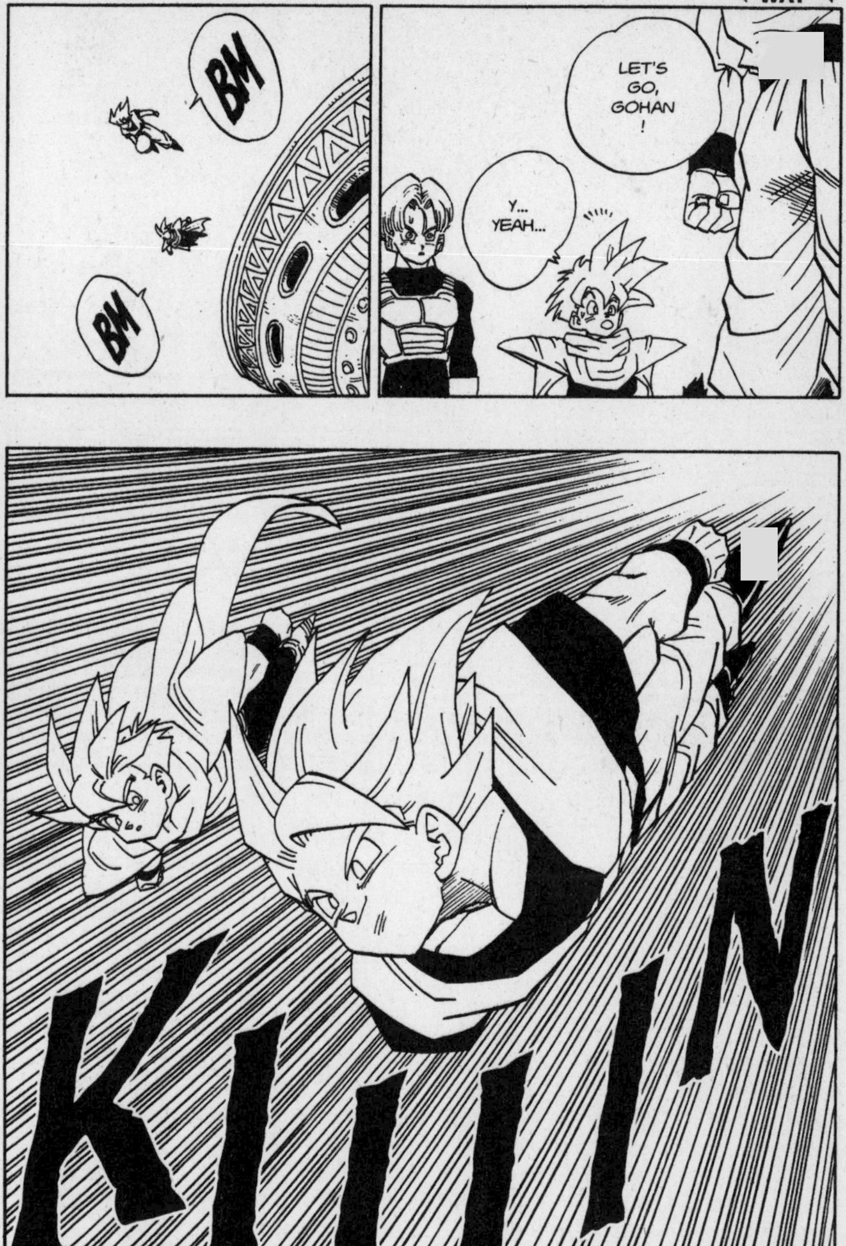

KIIIN

READ
THIS
WAY

COULD I MAKE A SHORT STOP HERE?

HYUU
HYUU

TP

READ THIS WAY

HELLO, MASTER KARIN !
N-NICE TO MEET YOU....!
MY. HOW YOU'VE GROWN.

HEY, YAJIROBE! YOU'RE BACK !

WHAT ARE YOU DOIN' HERE, GOKU... ?!
YOU BETTER NOT BE TRYIN' T'TALK ME INTO FIGHTIN' IN THAT STUPID TOURNAMENT !!

DON'T WORRY. THAT'S NOT WHY I'M HERE.
...ALTHOUGH I KNOW YOU MUST BE WISHIN' YOU COULD BEG F'R MY HELP...
G- GOOD...
EARTH IS IN DIRE STRAITS INDEED. TERROR...CHAOS...
I'VE NEVER SEEN ANYTHING LIKE CELL.
IN ITS COMPLETE FORM IT MIGHT BE THE PERFECT FIGHTER.

READ THIS WAY

...YOU'RE CERTAINLY CALM, CONSIDERING THAT.
I SUSPECT YOU MADE SOME VALUABLE DISCOVERY IN THE ROOM OF SPIRIT AND TIME.

HEH HEH HEH.
SORT OF.
WHAT...?! IS HE SERIOUS...?
...BUT I'VE BEEN WITH HIM THE WHOLE TIME...

MASTER KARIN, YOU'VE GOT A PRETTY GOOD IDEA HOW STRONG CELL IS BY WATCHING FROM HERE, RIGHT?
MM-HMM.
HE HASN'T SHOWN HIS TRUE POWERS, BUT I HAVE A SENSE.
CAN YOU COMPARE US?
I'M GONNA REV UP RIGHT NOW.

READ THIS WAY

...I ALWAYS THOUGHT IT TOOK A GIGANTIC EFFORT TO STAY IN SUPER SAIYAN STATE...BUT THEY LOOKED SO RELAXED...

THEY WERE SUPER SAIYANS, WITHOUT DOUBT.
SOMEHOW, THOUGH, THEY TRAINED THEMSELVES TO MAINTAIN THAT STATE AS IF IT WERE THEIR NORM.

THEN... DOES THAT MEAN...
...THEY'LL UNDERGO ANOTHER HUGE TRANSFORMATION DURING BATTLE... ?!

FOOL! WHERE ARE YOUR EYES?! YOUR EARS ?!
THEY DECIDED THAT THIS IS THEIR BEST COMBAT STATE! IF THEY GET USED TO IT, THEY'LL MINIMIZE THE STRAIN ON THEIR BODIES DURING BATTLE!

...

...KAKARROT HAS A STRATEGY...

HAH
!!!!
BOOM

READ THIS WAY

!!

YEEK !!!!

ENOUGH! YOU'RE GOING TO SHATTER THE TOWER!!!
EESH !!!

DOM
WH-WHAT'S THIS?!
THIS CHI... !!!

READ THIS WAY

IT'S...
IT'S GOKU... !!!

UNH... !!!!

WHEEZE *PANT*
WELL... !

THAT WAS ABOUT HALF POWER.
WHAT DO YOU THINK?

H-HALF POWER... ?!
YOU NEVER CEASE TO ASTOUND ME!
IS THERE NO LIMIT TO WHAT YOU CAN BECOME?!

THAT'S FUNNY ...
THAT CAN'T BE DAD'S FULL STRENGTH ...

BUT HOW AM I COMPARED TO CELL?!

HMM...
YOU ALWAYS ASK THE MOST DIFFICULT QUESTIONS...

AS I SAID, THIS IS ONLY SPECULATION...

BUT HONESTLY...
...I'M AFRAID CELL IS STILL A BIT STRONGER.

I THOUGHT SO.
I GUESSED RIGHT!
THANKS, MASTER KARIN!

OH GEEZ...
WHAT *IS* THIS CELL THING?!

READ THIS WAY

UH...
LET'S GO, GOHAN!
OH... YEAH. RIGHT.

S-SEE YOU LATER...!
PII

FFF
HUH?!

H-HE'S GONE...?!
HE AIN'T HUMAN NO MORE!

I TOLD HIM THAT HE DOESN'T SEEM TO STAND A CHANCE...AND HE SEEMED HAPPY! COULD HE SIMPLY BE ACCEPTING HIS FATE...?

JUST WHEN I THINK I'VE CAUGHT UP, HE WIDENS THE LEAD AGAIN... HE'LL PAY FOR THAT SOMEDAY!!

BLASTED KAKARROT...
IT'S ALWAYS LIKE THIS...
HE'S ALWAYS A STEP AHEAD OF ME... !!

PICCOLO!! GET YOUR TURN OVER WITH!! THERE'S A LINE BACKED UP OUT HERE!!

FFF

LET'S GRAB MOM AND GO HOME.
WE CAN REST BETTER THERE.

WE'LL REST 3 DAYS, TRAIN 3 DAYS, AND REST ANOTHER 3.
...THEN IT'LL BE TIME TO FIGHT.

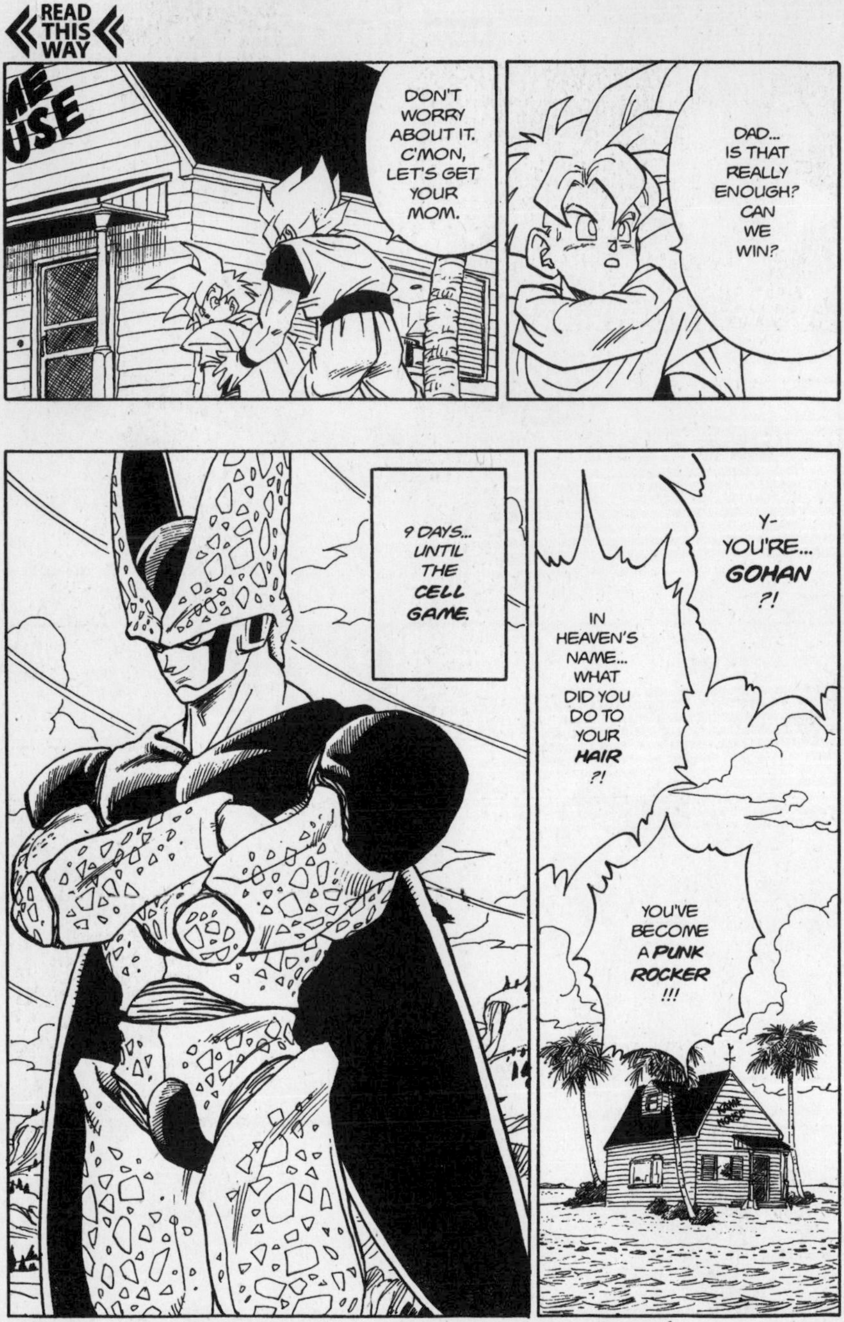

READ THIS WAY

DAD... IS THAT REALLY ENOUGH? CAN WE WIN?
DON'T WORRY ABOUT IT. C'MON, LET'S GET YOUR MOM.

Y- YOU'RE... **GOHAN** ?!

IN HEAVEN'S NAME... WHAT DID YOU DO TO YOUR **HAIR** ?!

YOU'VE BECOME A **PUNK ROCKER** !!!

9 DAYS... UNTIL THE ***CELL GAME.***

NEXT: The Royal Defense Force's Last Stand

DBZ: 198 • Cell vs. The Army

LOOK AT THE SIZE O' THE FISH IN THIS LAKE !

...

READ THIS WAY

DAD... ARE YOU SURE WE SHOULD BE RELAXING LIKE THIS?

DON'T YOU WORRY ABOUT A THING!
WE'LL PROBABLY BE FINE!

"P... PROB-ABLY"...?

TAKE IT EASY! WE'RE FINE!
LIKE I TOLD YOU, THERE'S NO POINT IN PUSHING ANY FURTHER. WE'VE TAKEN OUR BODIES AS FAR AS THEY CAN GO.

COME ON, GOHAN! FORGET WHAT'S COMIN' UP AND HAVE A GOOD TIME!

...

HEY YOU TWO! THE PICNIC'S READY!
HOORAY!

OOH, LOOKS YUMMY!
COULD YOU AT LEAST STOP BEING A SUPER SAIYAN WHILE WE EAT?
...

STORE
43
MOP-MOP SHA-BAM OOP-BOP

NOTHING'S OPEN. ALL THE STORES ARE CLOSED.
WELL, YEAH. WHO WANTS TO WORK WHEN THEY'RE GONNA DIE IN 7 DAYS?

WE INTERRUPT THIS PROGRAM FOR A SPECIAL NEWS REPORT.
THERE'S SOMEONE WORKING.

THE ROYAL DEFENSE FORCE IS AT THIS MOMENT RACING TO POINT 5, REGION 28, TO BRING DOWN THE MONSTER CALLED CELL. THEY ARE ABOUT TO LAUNCH THEIR ATTACK!
WHAT ?!

READ
THIS
WAY

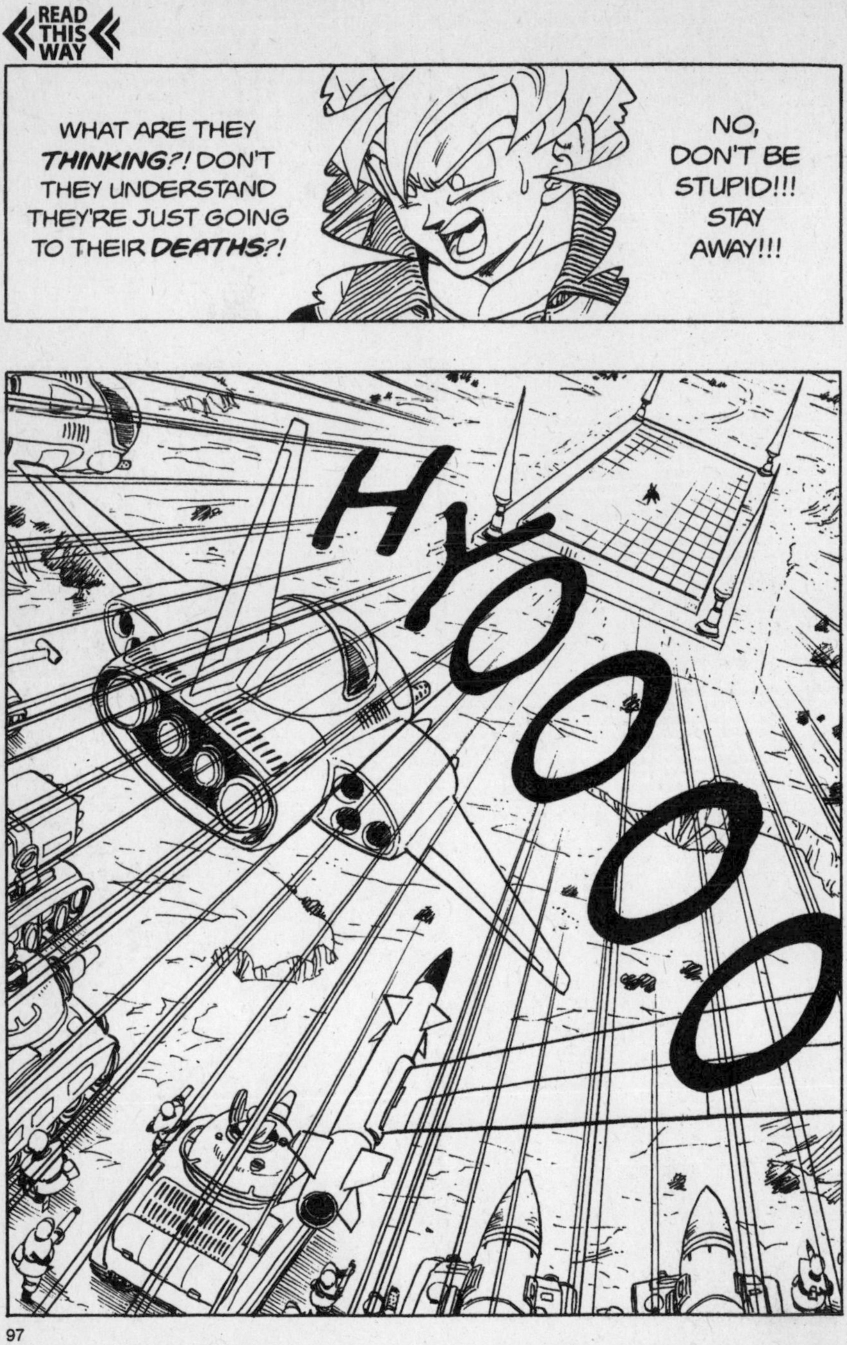

NO, DON'T BE STUPID!!! STAY AWAY!!!
WHAT ARE THEY *THINKING?!* DON'T THEY UNDERSTAND THEY'RE JUST GOING TO THEIR *DEATHS?!*
HYOOOO

READ THIS WAY

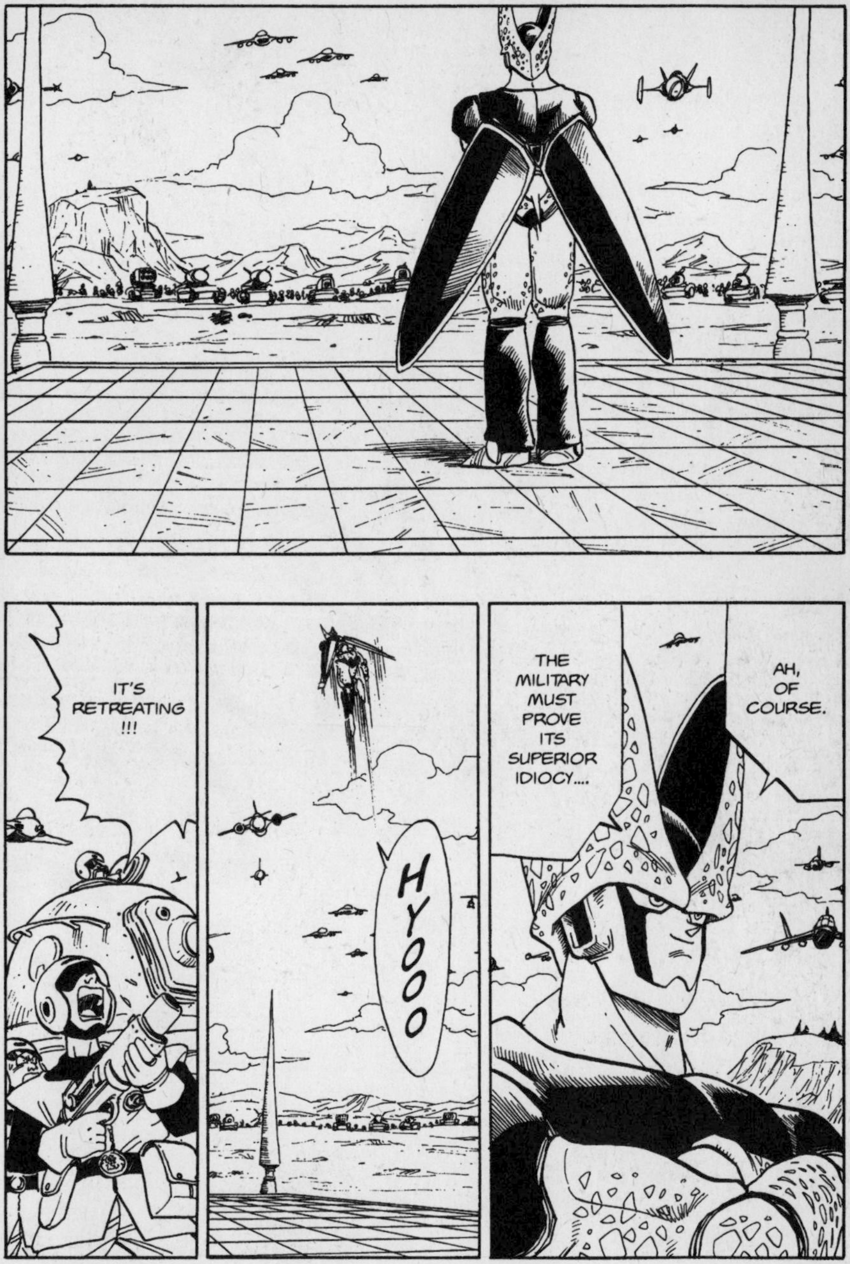

AH, OF COURSE.
THE MILITARY MUST PROVE ITS SUPERIOR IDIOCY....

HYOOO

IT'S RETREATING !!!

READ THIS WAY

TM

DON'T BE SILLY. I JUST DON'T WANT YOU TO DAMAGE MY PRETTY NEW ARENA.

WE HAVE IT PINNED!!! FIRE!!! FIRE!!!

READ THIS WAY

BOOM
BOOM
BOOM

WUMM
HOOO
K-BOOM
DMDMDM

READ THIS WAY

THIS IS AN ALL-OUT ATTACK!!! THE BLASTS ARE DEAFENING !!!

I'VE NEVER SEEN SUCH FIREPOWER!!! THEY'RE STILL NOT LETTING UP!!! SURELY NOTHING COULD SURVIVE THIS ONSLAUGHT!!!
GET OUT OF THERE— NOW!

ENOUGH !!!
HOLD YOUR FIRE !!!

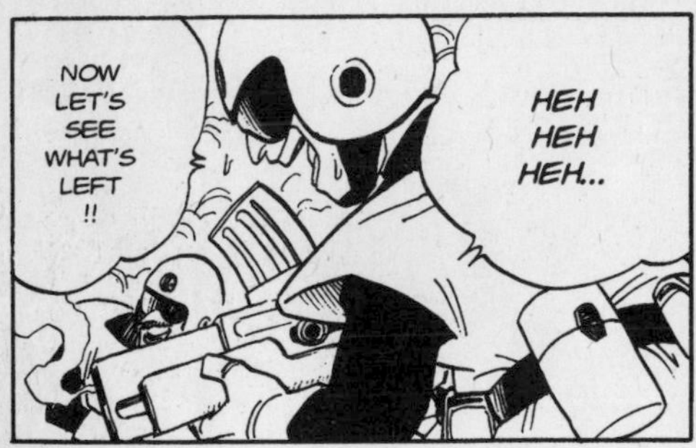
HEH HEH HEH...
NOW LET'S SEE WHAT'S LEFT !!

HYOOOO

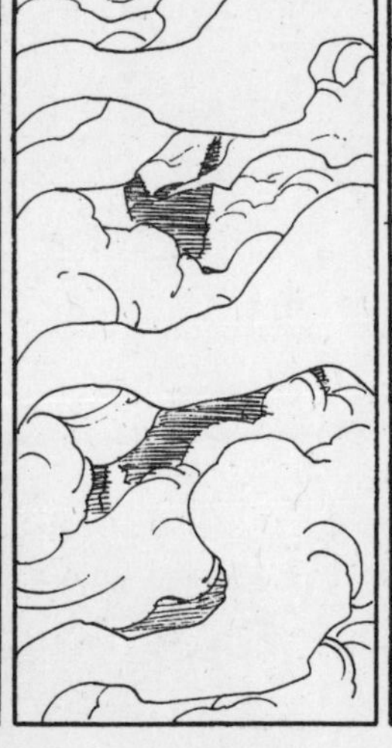

UH... ?!

IT...IT CAN'T BE...

STUPIDITY MUST NOT GO UNPUNISHED.

IT'S...IT'S ALIVE!! IT'S LIKE NOTHING HAPPENED... !

AIEEEE !!!

READ THIS WAY
HWA
B-B-B-BOOM

READ THIS WAY

ZZT... ZZAK... EEEEEE...

PCH

...
...NO...

HEH HEH HEH.

WELL, THAT KILLED... A FEW MINUTES.

READ THIS WAY

COULD YOU TWO GO ON HOME BY YOURSELVES? I'M SORRY. I HAVE TO SEE PICCOLO.

KCH

VNNN

HUH...?
WHAT WOULD HE NEED TO SEE PICCOLO FOR...?
...I DUNNO...

FFF

OH!
GOKU!
HEY.

READ THIS WAY

HEY...
PICCOLO! DID YOU GO IN THE ROOM OF SPIRIT AND TIME?
INDEED.

I CAN TELL!
YOU LOOK A LOT STRONGER!

WELL... DUH.

HMPH. I SUPPOSE I ASKED FOR THAT ONE...

SO WHAT DO YOU WANT HERE...?

UM...IS IT POSSIBLE FOR YOU AND KAMI-SAMA TO SPLIT IN TWO AGAIN?
WHAT?!

THE DRAGON BALLS DISAPPEARED BECAUSE YOU AND KAMI FUSED TOGETHER, RIGHT?

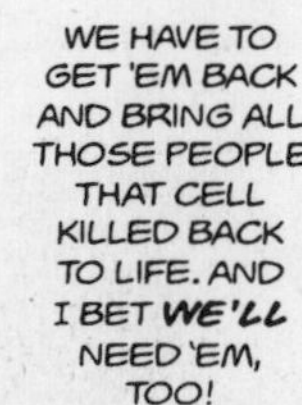
WE HAVE TO GET 'EM BACK AND BRING ALL THOSE PEOPLE THAT CELL KILLED BACK TO LIFE. AND I BET WE'LL NEED 'EM, TOO!

...WHY DON'T YOU JUST SAY IT?
I'VE GROWN MUCH STRONGER.. BUT I STILL CAN'T DO MUCH AGAINST CELL.

READ THIS WAY

YES, I SEE... UNFORTUNATELY, IT'S NOT POSSIBLE. ONCE MERGED, WE TWO CAN NEVER SEPARATE AGAIN.
THAT'S WHY I HESITATED SO MUCH BEFORE DOING IT.

YEAH... THAT'S KINDA...
...WHAT I FIGURED.
HEY, I HEARD FROM GOHAN THAT THE SURVIVING NAMEKIANS WENT TO ANOTHER PLANET!
MAYBE I'LL TRY LOOKING FOR THEM!

MAYBE ONE O' THEM WOULD BE WILLING TO COME LIVE ON EARTH!
HE CAN BECOME A GOD LIKE KAMI!! AND THE DRAGON BALLS WILL BE RESTORED!!

OH!!

DBZ: 199
The New Kami-sama

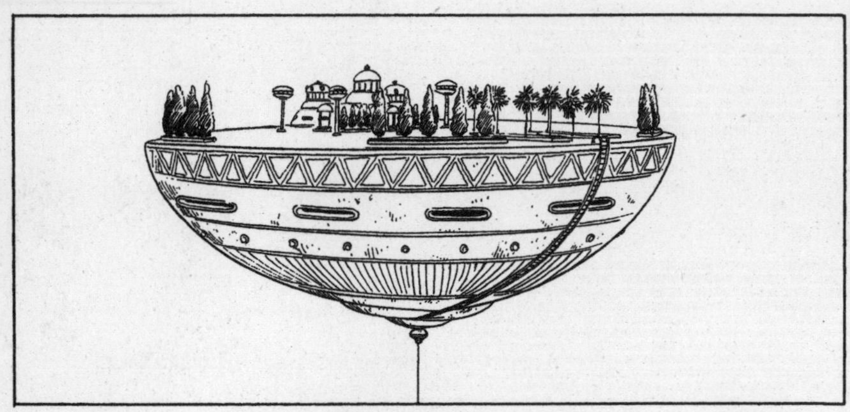

I'LL GO LOOK FOR THE NAMEKIANS RIGHT NOW!
POPO WILL BE SO HAPPY TO HAVE A NEW KAMI!
BUT GOKU, HOW WILL YOU DO THIS?
WE DON'T EVEN KNOW WHAT STAR SYSTEM THEY WENT TO. IT WILL TAKE TOO LONG!

READ THIS WAY

YOU'RE NOT THINKING!
I CAN TELEPORT, REMEMBER?!
I'LL JUST SCOUT FOR *CHI* SIMILAR TO YOURS!

YOU CAN FEEL *CHI*... FROM SO FAR AWAY?!
I THINK... IF IT'S NOT **TOO** FAR.

ANYWAY, I GOTTA TRY.
BE QUIET FOR A MINUTE...

GULP

READ THIS WAY

NOPE. THAT DIDN'T WORK.
NOW WHAT ?

I KNOW !!
I COULD LOOK OUT FROM THE LORD OF WORLDS' PLACE !

LEMME SEE...
THE LORD OF WORLDS...

IS... THIS GOING TO WORK... ?
I NEVER KNOW WITH HIM....

GOT HIM !!
FFF

READ THIS WAY

MY SUBJECTS... MY FRIENDS...

AS YOU SAW IN THE PREVIOUS BROADCAST, OUR MILITARY TURNED ALL ITS MIGHT AGAINST CELL... BUT WAS DECIMATED.
AS YOUR KING, THIS WAS MY RESPONSIBILITY.

I DEARLY WISH THERE HAD BEEN ANOTHER WAY...
BUT I COULD SEE NO OTHER.

AND NOW, I FEAR... THERE IS NOTHING ELSE TO BE DONE...
THOUGH WE CANNOT GIVE UP. WE MUST HOPE...

...HOPE THAT THERE WILL COME ANOTHER SAVIOR...LIKE THE BOY WHO DEFEATED THE ***DEMON KING PICCOLO*** LONG AGO!
LET US PRAY! LET US BEG OF THE GODS!

THERE'S ***ONE*** GOD WE DON'T HAVE ANYMORE...

READ
THIS
WAY

LET'S SEE...
WHERE'S HE HANGING OUT...?

OO! AH! AH!
HEY, BUBBLES!
HOW'VE YOU BEEN?

HO! LORD OF WORLDS!
WAKE UP! IT'S GOKU!

MM...?
GOKU?!

OOOO! IS THIS YOUR SUPER SAIYAN FORM?!
WHAT'S UP? JUST DROPPING IN FOR A VISIT?

FOR CRYIN' OUT LOUD—
ARE YOU FOR REAL?

DON'T YOU KNOW THE EARTH'S ABOUT TO BE WIPED OUT?!
HUH?!

HEY, WHAT AM I SUPPOSED TO DO?! I'M IN CHARGE OF A VAST AREA OF THE UNIVERSE HERE!!
I'M BUSY!! I CAN'T ALWAYS BE WATCHING EARTH!!

YOU WERE JUST TAKING A NAP.
IT'S TIRING DOING THIS!! ANYWAY... TELL ME ABOUT IT.

WELL...
B-BMP B-BMP

WHAT?!

...I HAVEN'T SAID ANYTHING YET.
WELL MAKE IT SNAPPY!

READ THIS WAY

BLAH BLAH BLAH..
UH-HUH... UH-HUH...

...AND THAT'S WHERE WE ARE.
I WAS WONDERING IF *YOU* KNEW WHERE THE NEW NAMEKIAN PLANET IS.

HMM, I SEE... YOU DO HAVE A PROBLEM...
YOU'RE REALLY A MAGNET FOR THESE THINGS, AREN'T YOU?

IT WOULD HELP IF I AT LEAST KNEW THE GENERAL DIRECTION.

I REALLY HOPE YOU FIND 'EM...

PIP

I'LL DO MY BEST.

MR. POPO'S BEEN LONELY WITHOUT KAMI-SAMA...

I CAN'T BLAME HIM... STUCK WAY UP THERE...

SHUT UP!! I CAN'T CONCENTRATE !!!

READ THIS WAY

OH!

I FOUND THEM!! THAT WAY!!
REALLY ?! THANKS !!

I MIGHT BE ABLE TO PICK UP THEIR *CHI* IF I AT LEAST KNEW WHICH WAY TO FOCUS.
WOW, TELEPORTATION!! WHEN DID YOU LEARN THAT?!

I'LL BET THE YARDRAT TAUGHT YOU...
AWFULLY CON-VENIENT, ISN'T IT...?

...
COULD YOU BE QUIET ?
YOU SEE WHAT IT'S LIKE ?!

!
THIS IS IT!! I'VE FOUND 'EM!!

FFF
AH!

READ
THIS
WAY

!!

WHAT...
WHAT THE...?!

WHOA...
ALL THESE PICCOLOS...

AND WHO...
...ARE *YOU?*

READ THIS WAY

UH...THE NAME'S SON GOKU, AND I COME FROM EARTH...

SON GOKU!! THE ONE WHO FOUGHT FREEZA ON PLANET NAMEK–
AND SAVED US ALL!!!

YEAH... *HEH*... EXCEPT THE PLANET BLEW UP...

BZZ BZZ
OO! AH!

...SO THAT'S THE STORY.
I WAS WONDERING IF ONE OF YOU COULD COME TO EARTH AND BECOME A **GOD**.

EARTH, EH?

WHY, THERE *IS* SOMEONE PERFECT FOR THE JOB....
REALLY?!

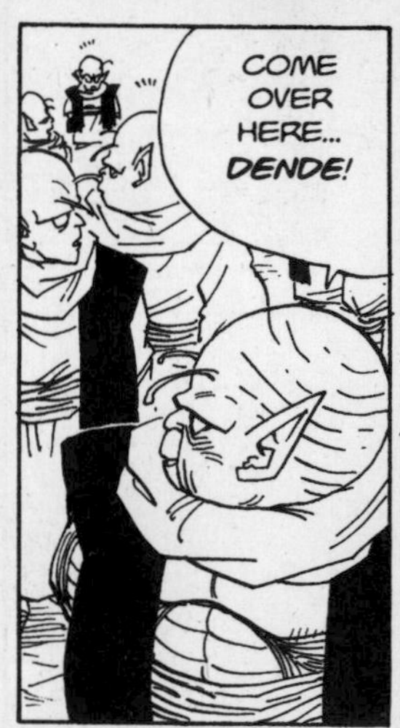
COME OVER HERE... **DENDE**!

READ THIS WAY

Y-YES SIR.

HE'S BEEN INFATUATED WITH EARTH EVER SINCE THEN. HE'S ALWAYS TALKING ABOUT HOW HE WANTS TO GO SEE GOHAN AND KURIRIN.

TH- THAT'S GREAT, BUT...
...YOU HAVE TO BE ABLE TO MAKE *DRAGON BALLS*.

DON'T WORRY. DENDE IS A TRUE SCION OF THE DRAGON CLAN!
HE'LL MAKE A FINE KAMI-SAMA!

THEN HE'S PERFECT!!
GREAT TO MEET YOU, DENDE!!

THANKS A LOT! WE'LL BE SURE TO TAKE GOOD CARE OF HIM!
GOOD LUCK.
GOODBYE, EVERYONE!
WE'LL PRAY FOR PEACE ON EARTH!

FFF

IT WORKED, LORD! HERE'S OUR NEW "GOD OF EARTH"!
SEE YA LATER!

VIII

DENDE!!

WAIT HERE! I'LL BRING OVER KURIRIN AND GOHAN!

READ THIS WAY

KAME HOUSE

THRILLING NEWS FOR THE PEOPLE OF EARTH!!

THE GREAT COMBATANT **HERCULE**--FORMERLY KNOWN AS THE WRESTLER "MR. SATAN"--HAS ANNOUNCED HE WILL ENTER THE **CELL GAME**!!

LET'S GIVE A BIG HAND FOR HERCULE!

WOO-HOO !!!
HER-CULE !! HER-CULE !!

WHO'S **HE**?
MARTIAL ARTS CHAMPION OF THE WORLD...

READ THIS WAY

CAN YOU HANDLE THIS, HERCULE?
CELL HAS JUST DESTROYED THE ROYAL MILITARY!

THAT WAS A GIMMICK. CELL SET UP BOMBS AHEAD OF TIME.
I COULD TELL RIGHT AWAY CELL'S AN AMATEUR WHEN IT COMES TO FIGHTING.

I SWEAR TO KNOCK THE BLUFF RIGHT OUT OF THAT CREEP!!!!
ARE YOU WITH ME?!

WOO-WOO!
HER-CULE! HER-CULE!
SLUR RRRP

OH BROTHER...
...ANOTHER DEAD IDIOT.

READ THIS WAY

OH, GOKU!
KURIRIN, COME WITH ME! I BROUGHT OUR NEW KAMI-SAMA! YOU REMEMBER DENDE?!
WHAT?! DENDE... THE NAMEKIAN?!

PAAA

IT *IS* HIM!!
HA HA!!

MAN, IT'S GOOD T'SEE YOU, DENDE!! CAN YOU BELIEVE THIS IS *GOHAN*?!
IS IT TRUE YOU'RE GONNA BE A GOD?!

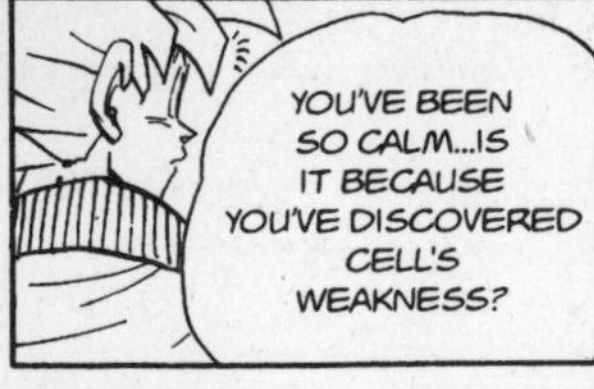
G-GOKU... CAN I ASK YOU SOMETHING?
YOU'VE BEEN SO CALM...IS IT BECAUSE YOU'VE DISCOVERED CELL'S WEAKNESS?

GEEZ...
DOES IT EVEN *HAVE* A WEAKNESS..?
......

NEXT: The Cell Game Begins

DBZ:200 • The Cell Game Begins!

DENDE... ARE YOU CERTAIN...
...THAT YOU CAN MAKE DRAGON BALLS?
HE'LL BE FINE !
THE GUY ON PLANET NAMEK SWEARS HE'S GREAT !
I'M SURE I CAN MAKE THE DRAGON BALLS IN... OH... 100 DAYS.
100 DAYS ?!
I-IT TAKES THAT LONG... ?!
OF COURSE, I CAN MAKE THEM RIGHT AWAY IF WE USE THE DRAGON BALLS YOU HAD ON EARTH THAT TURNED TO STONE!
WOO-HOO! PER-FECT !
SO DO WE GET THREE WISHES LIKE ON PLANET NAMEK ?!
UH-HUH.
WILL WE BE ABLE TO REVIVE MORE THAN ONE PERSON WITH A SINGLE WISH?
CAN WE SAY, "BRING BACK EVERYONE KILLED BY CELL" ?

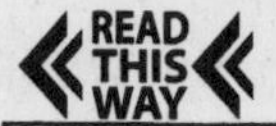
READ THIS WAY

HMM...WELL... THAT'S POSSIBLE IF I MAKE THEM THAT WAY...
BUT THEN WE'LL ONLY BE ABLE TO HAVE TWO WISHES.

WHAT?! THAT'S ALL IT TAKES...?

EXCELLENT. THEN DO IT.

FINE.
DO YOU HAVE THE MODEL OF THE DRAGON?
MR. POPO, BRING IT HERE.
YES, YES.

MR. POPO MADE THIS.
THAT'S AN... INTERESTING DRAGON.

KLUNK

...
MUMBLE MUMBLE

READ THIS WAY

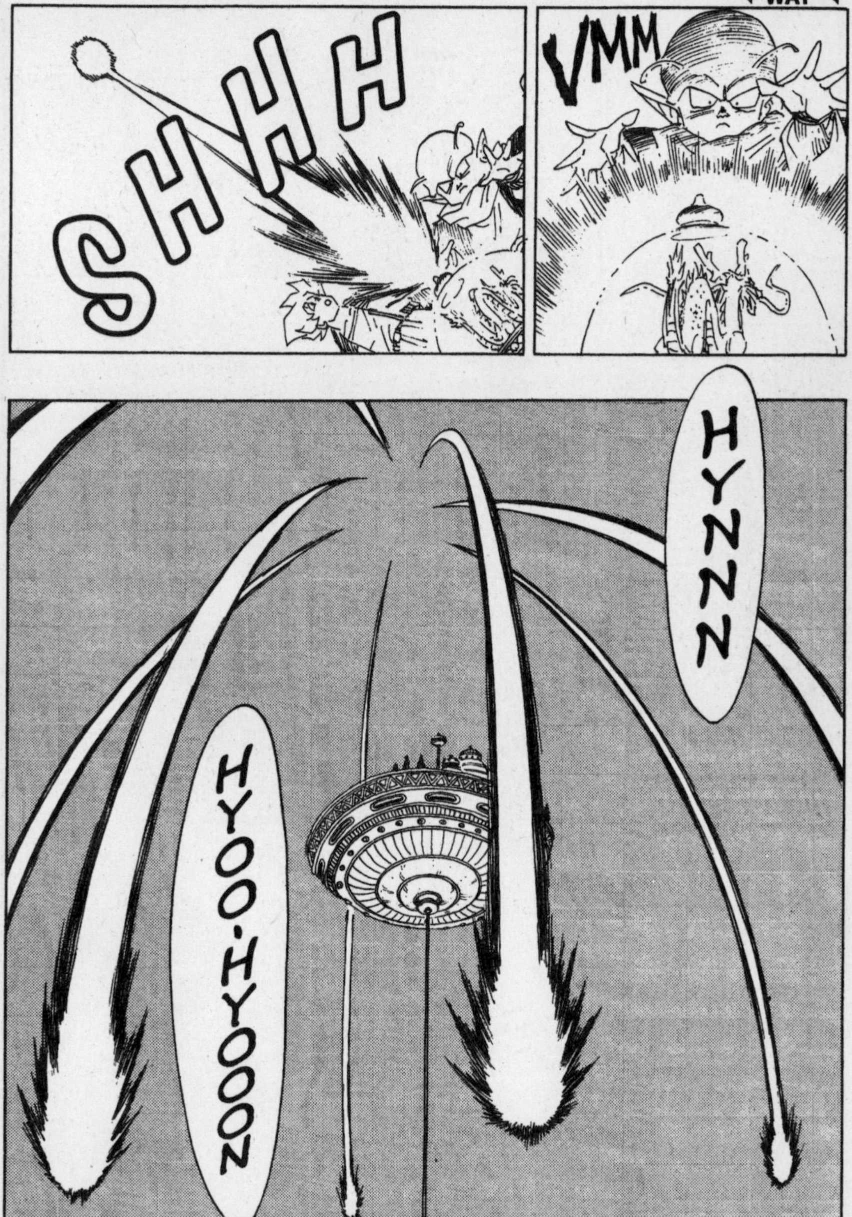

VMM

SHHHH

HYNNN

HYOO-HYOOOON

READ
THIS
WAY

THERE. THE DRAGON BALLS SHOULD BE BACK NOW.
WHAT ?!
AL-READY ?!

SPLENDID... *HEH*... HE IS TALENTED INDEED...

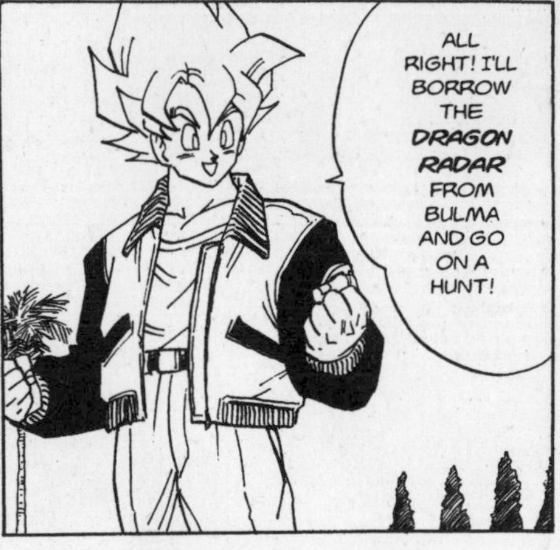
ALL RIGHT! I'LL BORROW THE **DRAGON RADAR** FROM BULMA AND GO ON A HUNT!

GOHAN, YOU DON'T HAVE TO TRAIN ANY MORE! STAY HERE WITH DENDE UNTIL THE **CELL GAME**!
WHAT ?!

BUT...
BUT DAD...

IT'LL BE FINE.
DON'T WORRY ABOUT IT.
SEE YA!

PFFF

READ THIS WAY

GOHAN... DO YOU KNOW WHAT HE'S THINKING? GOKU'S ALREADY SAID CELL IS STRONGER THAN HE IS, AND HE DOESN'T KNOW OF ANY WEAKNESSES...
...SO WHY IS HE SO CHEERFUL ?

UM...

HE WON'T TELL ME EITHER.
HE JUST TOLD ME TO LOOK FORWARD TO IT.

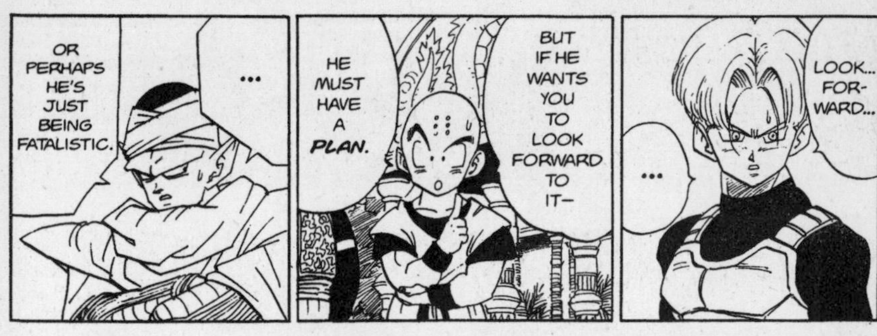
LOOK... FOR- WARD...
...
BUT IF HE WANTS YOU TO LOOK FORWARD TO IT—
HE MUST HAVE A *PLAN.*
...
OR PERHAPS HE'S JUST BEING FATALISTIC.

...

READ
THIS
WAY

AND SO...
THE CONSTRUCTION OF THIS ANDROID IS INCREDIBLE. DR. GERO WAS A JERK, BUT HE WAS A GENIUS JERK.
YEAH...

FOUND IT!!
THEY'RE REALLY BACK!!
WITH EACH OF THEM IN HIS OWN EMOTIONS...

TIME TICKED AWAY.
THIS IS BORING...
TEN DAYS WAS MUCH TOO LONG...

READ THIS WAY

GREAT!
NOW WE HAVE ALL SEVEN!
ELSEWHERE, **HERCULE**, MARTIAL ARTS CHAMPION, BECAME FAMOUS AS THE HERO ABOUT TO FACE CELL...
NEWS
HERCULE
EARTH'S MIGHTIEST WARRIOR
UNTIL FINALLY, THE DAWN OF M___ THE 17TH ARRIVED...

ALL RIGHTY !!
TIME TO GO!
GG
GW
TUG

READ THIS WAY

BE CAREFUL, GOKU. DON'T GET KILLED.
I KNOW, I KNOW.

AND GOHAN'S **NOT** FIGHTING! ***RIGHT?!***
HUH ?!

OH... UM...
SWEAR TO ME—
THAT YOU WON'T LET HIM FIGHT !!

I BETTER GET GOING !!
HEY !!

PFFF

...HE ***IS*** GOING TO FIGHT.
OH, GOHAN...

READ THIS WAY

HERE HE IS!

IT'S FINALLY TIME.
HUH? WHERE'S VEGETA ?

HE WENT ON AHEAD...

OH-HO.
RARIN' TO GO, HUH?
HE MUST'VE GOTTEN A LOT BETTER.

WHAT'S WRONG WITH EVERYBODY..? YOU'RE NOT NERVOUS, ARE YOU?

G-GOKU... THERE'S BAD NEWS...
WE CAN HAVE LOTS OF PEOPLE COME BACK TO LIFE LIKE WE SAID...
BUT THIS TIME... PEOPLE WHO DIED ONCE CAN'T COME BACK AGAIN.

I'M SORRY...
I SHOULD'VE SAID SO AT THE BEGIN-NING.

READ THIS WAY

OH, DON'T WORRY ABOUT IT, DENDE!
WE'LL JUST HAVE TO NOT DIE!
N-NOT DIE...?
TH-THIS IS **CELL** WE'RE TALKING ABOUT!
COME ON, LET'S GET GOING!
OR WE WON'T MAKE IT BY NOON!

HWOOO---

THE DAY HAS COME...
I CAN'T WAIT UNTIL YOU'RE HERE...SON GOKU.

READ
THIS
WAY

20 MORE MINUTES UNTIL THE CELL GAME THAT WILL DECIDE THE FATE OF THE EARTH!
SPECTATORS HAVE STAYED AWAY, FEARING FOR THEIR OWN SAFETY!
ZTV

AS YOU CAN SEE, CELL HAS NOT MOVED AN INCH! HE'S JUST STANDING IN THE MIDDLE OF THE RING!
EARTH'S HERO HERCULE STILL HASN'T...

WAIT!

KRIII
THAT CAR...

IT'S HIM!! HERCULE IS HERE!!!

READ
THIS
WAY

OOO!!! LOOK AT HIM
PUMP HIS FIST
AT THE CAMERA!!
HE KNOWS THE
WHOLE WORLD IS
WATCHING HIM!!!

WOO!
WOO!
HER-
CULE
!
HER-
CULE
!

VWOOM

HEH
HEH
HEH...

READ THIS WAY

SNAP
NKH
OHHH YEAH!!! HERCULE HAS JUST ANNOUNCED THAT THE MATCH IS ON!!!

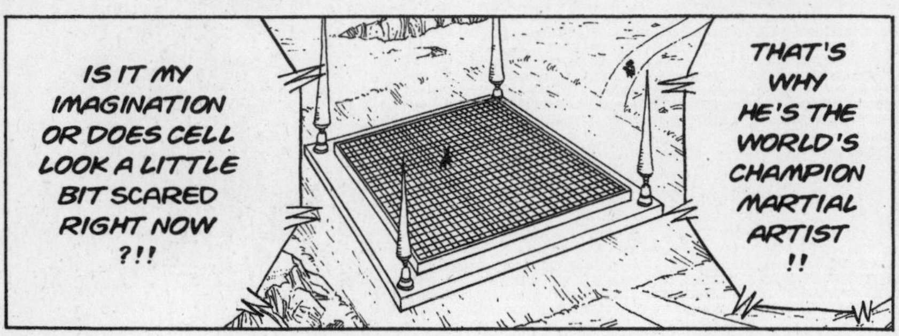
THAT'S WHY HE'S THE WORLD'S CHAMPION MARTIAL ARTIST !!
IS IT MY IMAGINATION OR DOES CELL LOOK A LITTLE BIT SCARED RIGHT NOW ?!!

...
...WHAT IS THAT LITTLE INSECT... ?
WE'RE DOWN TO 15 MINUTES 'TIL THE CELL GAME BEGINS !!
IT'S CELL VS. HERCULE!!! AND I THINK WE'LL SEE HERCULE STANDING IN THE END!!!

NEXT: *The Whole Team Arrives!*

DBZ: 201 • Heroes Assemble!

THERE ARE STILL 12 MINUTES 'TIL THE CELL GAME BEGINS—
BUT HE'S ALREADY STEPPING UP TO THE RING!!!

THIS BOY IS READY!!! HE'S THE MAN WE CAN COUNT ON!!!

READ THIS WAY

KWIF KWIF

HUH ?!

IS HE TELLING US...
TO JOIN HIM DOWN THERE... ?

NOD NOD

W-WELL... *UH*... THIS IS ODD, BUT...

ALL *RIGHT*!! WE'LL TAKE HIM UP ON IT!!! WE'RE *PROS*, AREN'T WE?! LET'S SHOW 'IM WHAT WE'RE *MADE* OF!!
W-WE'RE SAFE WITH HERCULE ANYWAY !!
ZIP

CAN YOU FEEL THE *TENSION* THROUGH THE CAMERA ?
THE *BRAVEST* REPORTER ON *EARTH* IS APPROACHING THE RING THAT WILL DETERMINE THE WORLD'S FUTURE!

UMM... SHOULD I STEP INTO THE RING, TOO... ?
I'M HERE. DON'T WORRY.

READ THIS WAY

H-HOW ARE YOU FEELING RIGHT NOW, HERCULE?

I FEEL SORRY FOR CELL. IT TALKED SO BIG. BUT IT NEVER KNEW THAT ANYBODY AS STRONG AS ME EXISTED.
WELL, IT'S TOO LATE TO TAKE ANY OF IT BACK NOW!

LISTEN, CELL! I KNOW YOUR SECRET!
YOU DESTROYED THE CITY AND THE MILITARY WITH BOMBS!!
BUT I'VE SEEN THROUGH YOUR TRICK!!

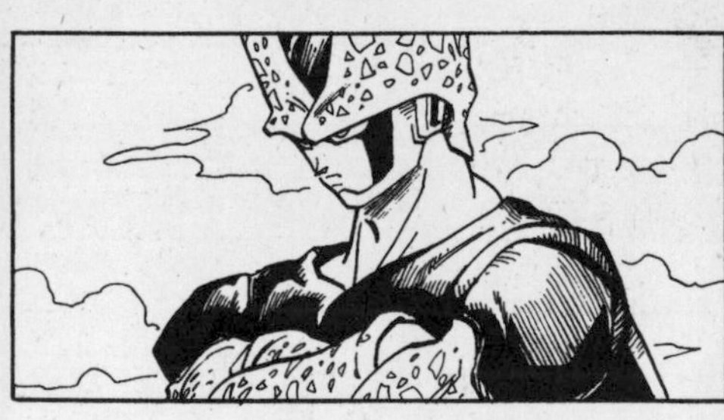

IT'S PRETENDING NOT TO LISTEN.
HEH HEH HEH...
IT'S TOO SCARED TO FACE THE TRUTH.
HA HA HA!
I'LL STICK MY TONGUE OUT AT HIM!

READ THIS WAY

WAH HA HA!! THEN I'LL MOON HIM!
PAT PAT

WOO! YAY!
HA HA HA!!! GO, HERCULE !!
2TV

...
I WOULDN'T MIND IF HE GOT KILLED...

HUH ?!

WH... WHAT... ?!
WHAT'S THE MATTER ?

KIIIIIN
WH-WHAT IS THAT... ?

VEGETA. I SHOULD'VE KNOWN HE WOULDN'T LEARN.
HE'D BETTER HAVE IMPROVED A LITTLE.

READ
THIS
WAY

TP

UM... A WEIRD-LOOKING MAN JUST SHOWED UP...

I ALMOST THOUGHT HE FLEW THROUGH THE AIR...
MUST BE A TRICK.

I-IS HE PLANNING TO TAKE PART IN THE CELL GAME, TOO...?
L-LET'S GO ASK HIM...

READ THIS WAY

UM... YOU KNOW, IT'S PRETTY DANGEROUS TO BE WATCHING FROM THIS CLOSE...

GET LOST.
AND DON'T TALK TO ME AGAIN.

...

...OBVIOUSLY SOME KIND OF NUT.
HIS HAIR'S WEIRD TOO.
SIGH... THOSE KINDS OF PEOPLE CAUSE THE MOST TROUBLE.

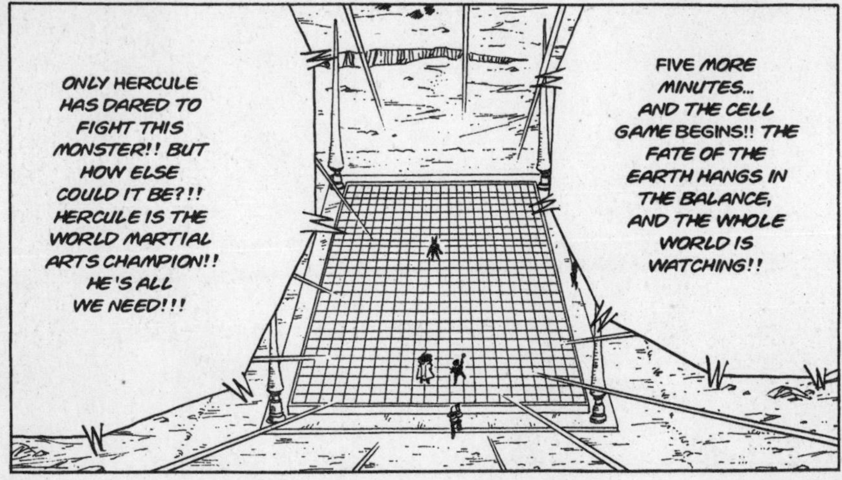
FIVE MORE MINUTES... AND THE CELL GAME BEGINS!! THE FATE OF THE EARTH HANGS IN THE BALANCE, AND THE WHOLE WORLD IS WATCHING!!
ONLY HERCULE HAS DARED TO FIGHT THIS MONSTER!! BUT HOW ELSE COULD IT BE?!! HERCULE IS THE WORLD MARTIAL ARTS CHAMPION!! HE'S ALL WE NEED!!!

READ THIS WAY

TMM
HUH ?!

D-DID HE JUST FLY TOO...?
H-HE MUST'VE USED THE SAME TRICK...

WHAT A SURPRISE. NO. 16.
I DIDN'T THINK YOU WERE STILL AROUND. YOU'VE BEEN REPAIRED, I SEE.

...
ONLY BULMA AND HER FATHER COULD REPAIR SUCH A ROBOT... WHAT A WASTE OF EFFORT...

READ THIS WAY

...CELL TALKED TO HIM... DO THEY KNOW EACH OTHER...?
WH-WHO CARES? HE DOESN'T LOOK LIKE MUCH, ANYWAY...

PWIK

HE'S HERE. SON GOKU... I'VE BEEN WAITING FOR YOU.

H-HEY... LOOK OVER THERE...
HUH?

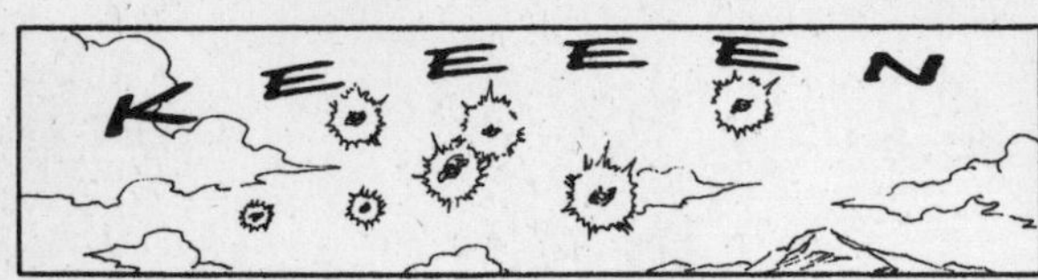

KEEEEN

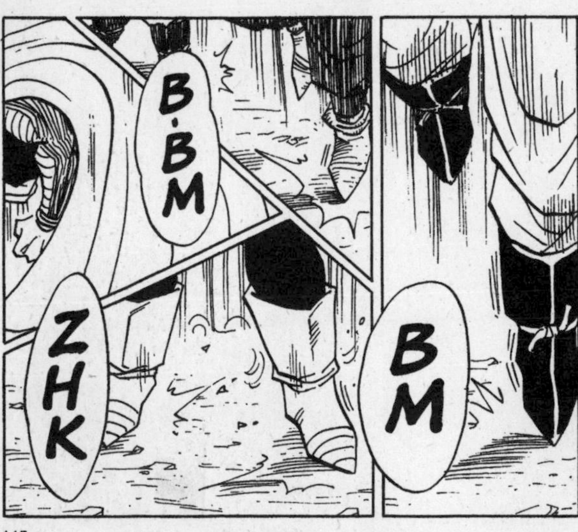

BM
B·BM
ZHK

亀

READ THIS WAY

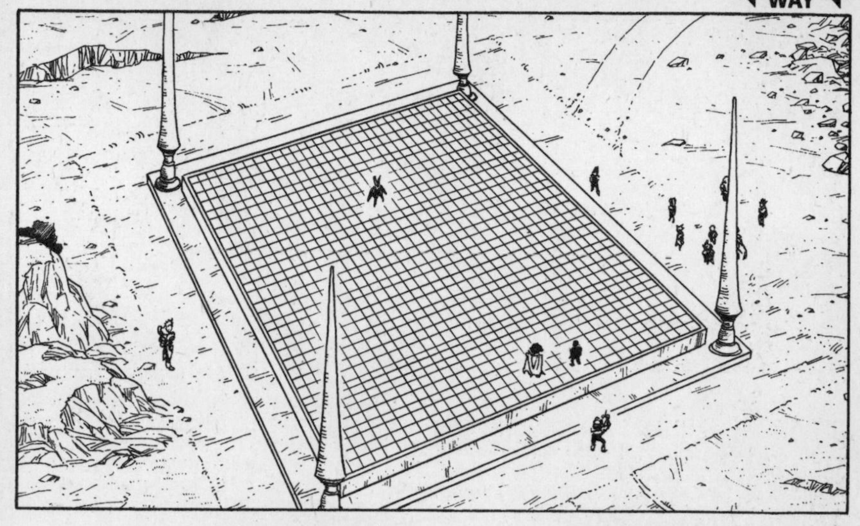

WELCOME, EVERYONE.

FEH...
WHAT'S THE POINT IN BRINGING *THEM* ALONG ?

...THEY... THEY ALL *FLEW* IN...
M-MUST BE A POPULAR TRICK...

READ THIS WAY

HEY !
IT'S #16! GUESS HE GOT REPAIRED.

I WANTED TO THANK YOU, KURIRIN.
I OWE IT TO YOU THAT I'M BACK IN ACTION.

HEY... GLAD TO DO IT!

LET'S DO OUR BEST.

I WAS CREATED TO KILL YOU, SON GOKU.
DON'T EVER FORGET THAT.

MAN... THAT'S A DOWNER...

...
THESE GUYS ARE STEALING MY SHOW...

READ THIS WAY

WELL THEN !
FLEX
MIND IF I START US OFF?
WHAT ?!

DO YOU REALLY THINK WE SHOULD START WITH YOU...?

IS IT OKAY, VEGETA ?

DO WHAT YOU WANT.
I'LL STILL BE THE ONE TO FINISH HIM.

...

HEY...
WHO SAID YOU GET TO PICK ?!!!

READ THIS WAY

UM, EXCUSE ME...
ARE YOU ALL ENTERING THE CELL GAME?
YUP. MOST OF US, ANYWAY.

YOU'VE GOT TO BE KIDDING !!
THIS ISN'T A GAME !!
I MEAN, YEAH, IT'S CALLED A "GAME," BUT IT'S—

YOU'RE THE ONE WHO DOESN'T GET IT.

HEH HEH HEH... I DIDN'T EXPECT THIS...
I GUESS SOME PEOPLE'VE BEEN LIVING UNDER A ROCK AND NEVER HEARD OF HERCULE !

THIS IS THE WORLD CHAMPION MARTIAL ARTIST!! THE MIGHTIEST IN THE WORLD !!

GOKU, JUST LET HIM GO FIRST.
WELL...IF YOU SAY SO...

IT'S TIME.

NEXT: The Cell Game's Handicap!!

DBZ:202 · Hercule, Champion of the World

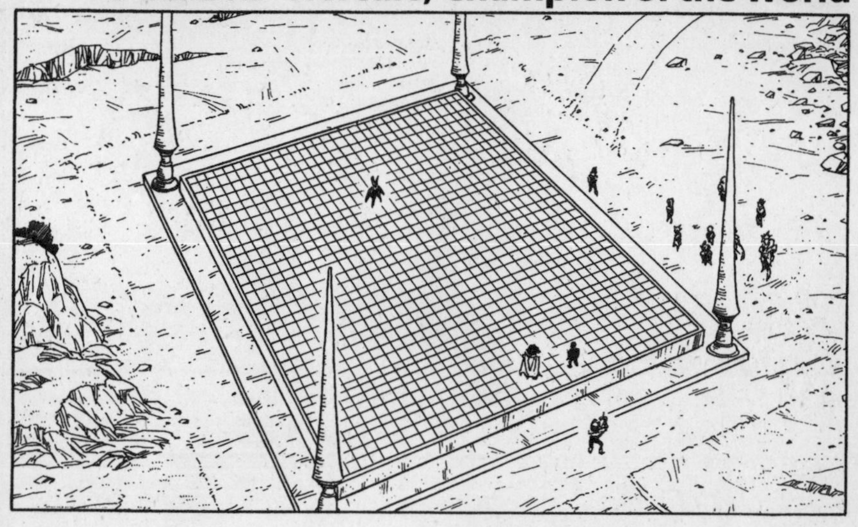

I'M FIRST, OF COURSE.
THE OBVIOUS CHOICE.
I DON'T CARE WHO GOES FIRST.
GET UP HERE.

READ THIS WAY

YOU'LL GET KILLED.
I'M SAYING THIS FOR YOUR OWN GOOD— GO HOME!

SIGH...

HEY, GET A SHOT OF THAT IDIOT.
SURE.

I CAN ALMOST HEAR THE WHOLE WORLD GROANING.
DID YOU HEAR WHAT THIS MAN JUST SAID TO HERCULE?

HE HAD THE GALL TO SAY, "YOU'LL GET KILLED!" TO TELL HERCULE TO GO HOME!!

READ THIS WAY

BOOO BOOO
GET OUTTA THERE, JERK!!!

AT THE KING'S CASTLE...

WELL, WHAT CAN YOU DO WITH A FOOL?
HE STILL DOESN'T APPRECIATE HERCULE'S GREATNESS AFTER BEING TOLD!!

HONEST-LY.
THESE PEOPLE ARE SO DIFFICULT...

HE REMINDS ME... OF THE BOY WHO SAVED US ALL FROM THE DEMON KING PICCOLO LONG AGO...

...BUT THE COLOR OF HIS EYES AND HAIR WERE DIFFERENT... IT CAN'T BE HIM...

AND YET... THE ONE WHO'S STANDING WITH THEM...
CAN HE POSSIBLY BE THE DEMON KING PICCOLO HIMSELF...?

READ THIS WAY

JUST LET THE IDIOT HAVE HIS WAY.
WE'LL BRING 'IM BACK TO LIFE WITH THE DRAGON BALLS.

SHEESH.
FINE...

WELL! A MOMENT OF WISDOM!
ALTHOUGH I'M SURE THE FOOL DOESN'T REALIZE HE'S JUST ESCAPED CERTAIN DEATH! HA HA!

HERCULE IS CLEARLY ANNOYED AT THE DISRUPTION.
HE FINALLY GETS HIMSELF READY FOR THE MATCH!!
TUG

FWOP

HE TAKES OFF HIS CAPE...
AND HIS GLORIOUS CHAMPION'S BELT!!!

READ
THIS
WAY

THE CELL GAME IS ABOUT TO BEGIN!!!

THE FATE OF THE EARTH RIDES ON THIS, BUT OUR CHAMPION, HERCULE, TOLD US THAT HE'S BEEN LOOKING FORWARD TO THIS DAY!!

WHAT'S THIS? HERCULE...
...IS TAKING SOMETHING FROM HIS POCKET?
KCH

IT'S A CAPSULE!! HE'S GOT A CAPSULE!!
BOM

AND IT'S A DUFFEL BAG!!
A HUGE DUFFEL BAG CAME OUT OF THE CAPSULE!!

READ THIS WAY

ZZZIP
AND INSIDE THAT BAG IS...

TILES?!! IT'S FILLED WITH TILES ?!!
CHK
HERCULE IS PUTTING THEM INTO A NEAT STACK !

I DON'T BELIEVE THIS...
DON'T TELL ME...

HE'S DONE !!!
ONE, TWO, THREE... 15!! 15 IN ALL !!!
15 TILES HAVE BEEN PILED HIGH !!!

HEH HEH HEH...

HUFF
HE'S CONCENTRATING!! HERCULE IS GATHERING ALL HIS STRENGTH!!!

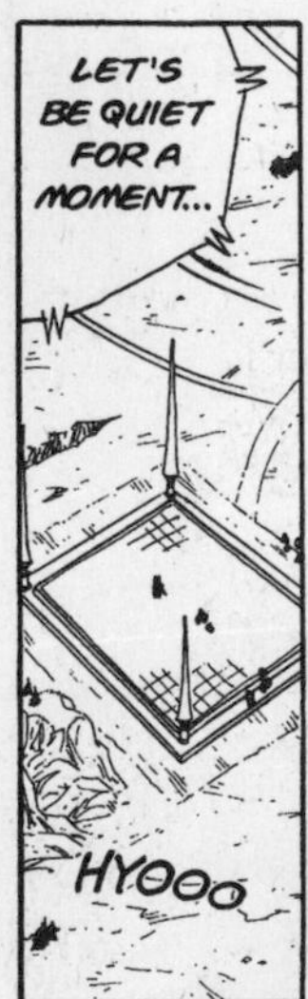
LET'S BE QUIET FOR A MOMENT...
HYOOO

READ THIS WAY

HSSS
RR-
RR-
AAH...
!!
K-K-K-K-K-K

READ THIS WAY

OH NO!! ONE DIDN'T BREAK !!!
BUT WHAT A FEAT!!! WHAT POWER !!!
14!! 14 TILES HAVE BEEN SMASHED TO PIECES!!

PHEW !
THROB THROB

WOO-HOO! YEAH !
YAY
AWESOME !!!
YAY
HERCULE, YOU'RE AMAZING !!!

DUHHHH

.....
WHAT A MORON...

READ THIS WAY

CELL!!!

LOOK AT THESE TILES!!!

THIS IS WHAT YOU'LL LOOK LIKE...
...ONE MINUTE FROM NOW!

WOO-HOO!!!
YOU TELL 'IM! HER-CULE, HER-CULE!

AMAZING!!! WHAT A MOMENT THAT WAS!!!
I SHALL NEVER FORGET IT!

READ
THIS
WAY

THAT WAS PERFECT!! IT WORKED OUT JUST LIKE I WANTED!!!

B-BMP B-BMP

I'M GLAD I SET MY VCR TO RECORD THIS!!

CELL MUST BE TERRIFIED!! THE ONCE ARROGANT MONSTER MUST BE CRINGING NOW AT HERCULE'S DESTRUCTIVE POWER!!!

BUT IT'S TOO LATE TO APOLOGIZE!!! THE PEOPLE OF THE WORLD WON'T PARDON ITS CRIMES!!!

ALL RIGHT, THEN!! COME AT ME!!!

READ
THIS
WAY

THE CELL GAME HAS BEGUN!! WILL THE WORLD LIVE OR DIE?!!
HERCULE, UNRIVALED WINNER OF THE WORLD CHAMPIONSHIP, VS. CELL!! NOW THE FISTS OF HERCULE WILL DOLE OUT JUSTICE!!

HER-CULE!
HER-CULE!

THE RULES ARE SIMPLE!! YOU LOSE IF YOU FALL OUT OF BOUNDS, GIVE UP, OR DIE!!
WE'RE WITH YOU, HERCULE!! WE KNOW YOU'RE GOING TO KILL HIM!!

HY AAAH!!!
VSH

READ THIS WAY

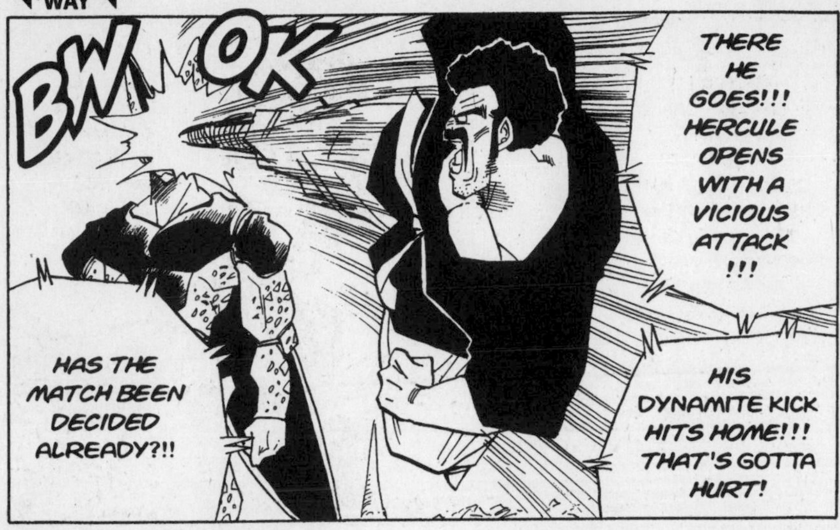
BWOK
THERE HE GOES!!! HERCULE OPENS WITH A VICIOUS ATTACK!!!
HIS DYNAMITE KICK HITS HOME!!! THAT'S GOTTA HURT!
HAS THE MATCH BEEN DECIDED ALREADY?!!

HERCULE DOESN'T EASE UP HIS BARRAGE OF BLOWS!!
CELL IS HELPLESS!! IT CAN'T EVEN FIGHT BACK!!
THOK
WAK
BAM BAM
HERCULE IS TOO MUCH FOR THE MONSTER!!!

BWA HA HA HA HA!!!

GET OUT OF MY FACE.
WAP

KONG

HUH ?

PHEW...
I WAS ACTUALLY ROOTING FOR CELL FOR A MINUTE...

UH...
URK...
OW !
OWWWW !!

HE LIVED... PITY.
I SUPPOSE NOT EVEN CELL WANTS TO DIRTY ITS HANDS ON SOMETHING LIKE THAT.
...

SHHHH
ZTV

HE... HE FELL OUT OF BOUNDS...
UM... ER...
HERCULE... HAS LOST...

READ THIS WAY

COME ON NOW. LET'S GET THIS GAME STARTED.
WHO'S GOING FIRST? YOU, SON GOKU?

YUP.
THAT'S RIGHT.

D-DOES THIS MEAN...
THE EARTH IS NOW **DOOMED**...?

OW.
OW OW OW...

H-HERCULE... HOW COULD YOU LOSE?
I...UH... I JUST LOST MY FOOTING!

IT LOOKED LIKE YOU GOT KNOCKED THROUGH THE AIR...
DON'T WORRY... I'LL TAKE A LITTLE BREAK AND THEN I'LL **REALLY** GET DOWN TO BUSINESS!

HE STILL DOESN'T REALIZE...?
HE'S THE WORLD CHAMPION **IDIOT**!

TO BE CONTINUED IN **DRAGON BALL Z** VOL. 18!

DRAGON BALL TRUNKS THE STORY

ドラゴンボール／トランクス ザ ストーリー

とりやまあきら 鳥山明 BIRD STUDIO

The Lone Warrior (Side Story)

IN THE FUTURE...

DG DGOOM
HYAH!!
HAH!!

HF
HF
GOOD, TRUNKS!
THAT'S ENOUGH FOR TODAY!

READ
THIS
WAY

YOU'VE IMPROVED A LOT, TRUNKS.
HF
HF
YOU MIGHT EVEN LEAVE ME IN THE DUST IN A FEW MONTHS.

IF ONLY THE *SENZU* PLANT HADN'T DIED OUT, YOU COULD'VE GOTTEN YOUR ARM BACK.
YEAH... BUT WHAT'S GONE IS GONE, RIGHT ?

I'M JUST GLAD I COULD ESCAPE AT ALL.

YOU KNOW WHAT MOM SAID, GOHAN ?
IT STARTLES HER EVERY TIME SHE SEES YOU IN THAT *GI*, 'CAUSE YOU LOOK SO MUCH LIKE YOUR DAD !
CAPSULE CORP.

I MADE IT HOPING IT WOULD MAKE ME AS STRONG AS DAD WAS BEFORE HE DIED...
BUT I GUESS IT'S NOT JUST THE CLOTHES.
HA HA...

READ THIS WAY

!!

D-DOOM

OH NO !!!
THE ANDROIDS... !!! THEY'RE BACK !!!
CAPSULE CORP.

THE CITY... !!!

DOOM
BMMM

READ THIS WAY

NO...
D-DOON
I...I CAN'T LET THEM DO THIS ANYMORE... !!

ZSH

HYAH !!!!

READ
THIS
WAY

B-BUT GOHAN, NOT WITH ONE ARM... !!
TRUNKS, STAY RIGHT HERE, YOU HEAR ME?!

NO! I'M GOING IF YOU ARE !!!
I'VE GOTTEN A LOT STRONGER !!!
CAPSUL

LOOK !!
HUH ?!

WG

FMP

IF YOU DIE TOO, THERE WON'T BE ANYBODY LEFT TO PROTECT THE EARTH.
YOU'RE THE LAST ONE WITH A CHANCE TO BEAT THOSE ANDROIDS SOMEDAY.

READ THIS WAY

BM

DOOM

VP

READ
THIS
WAY

DOOM
ENOUGH, 17. THERE AREN'T MANY MORE HUMANS LEFT HERE.
LET'S GO SOMEWHERE ELSE. THERE MUST BE A LOT OF THEM HIDING UP NORTH.

LET'S TAKE OUR TIME. THE FUN'LL BE OVER IF WE EXTERMINATE THEM ALL AT ONCE.

YEAH... BUT THINK HOW MUCH FUN WE'LL HAVE WHILE IT LASTS!
UH... AHH...

THEN LET'S PLAY THAT GAME AGAIN--WHERE WE RUN THEM DOWN WITH CARS.
WOOM
ZAP

READ THIS WAY

THOK

HWOG

K-KRASH

READ THIS WAY

TOK

HA HA HA HA HA!!

I LIKED THIS OUTFIT. MAKES ME MAD TO GET HOLES IN IT...
I ONLY HAVE 4 SETS OF THIS OUTFIT LEFT. CLOTHES AREN'T AS TOUGH AS OUR BODIES, YOU KNOW!

IT'S BEEN A WHILE, SON GOHAN. A WHOLE YEAR, HASN'T IT?
I'M AMAZED YOU ESCAPED ALIVE AFTER ALL THAT...

I'VE BEEN TRAINING HARD. YOU WON'T BEAT ME THIS TIME.
IT'S YOUR TURN TO LOSE!

READ THIS WAY

OUR TURN? ...HEH HEH HEH... SORRY TO DISAPPOINT...

BUT I DIDN'T EVEN USE HALF MY POWER LAST TIME.

!!

...WHAT...?!

I WON'T LET YOU ESCAPE THIS TIME...

YOU'RE DEAD!

VWNN

TEE HEE...

READ THIS WAY

UNH...
OH !!
G-
GOHAN... ?!
I...I DON'T FEEL HIM... !!
GOHAN'S CHI IS GONE... !!
!!

READ
THIS
WAY

APSULE
CORP.

THREE YEARS PASS...

MOM, I'M HOME.
KRIII
I GOT US A LOT OF GOOD FOOD TODAY.
TAE FOODS

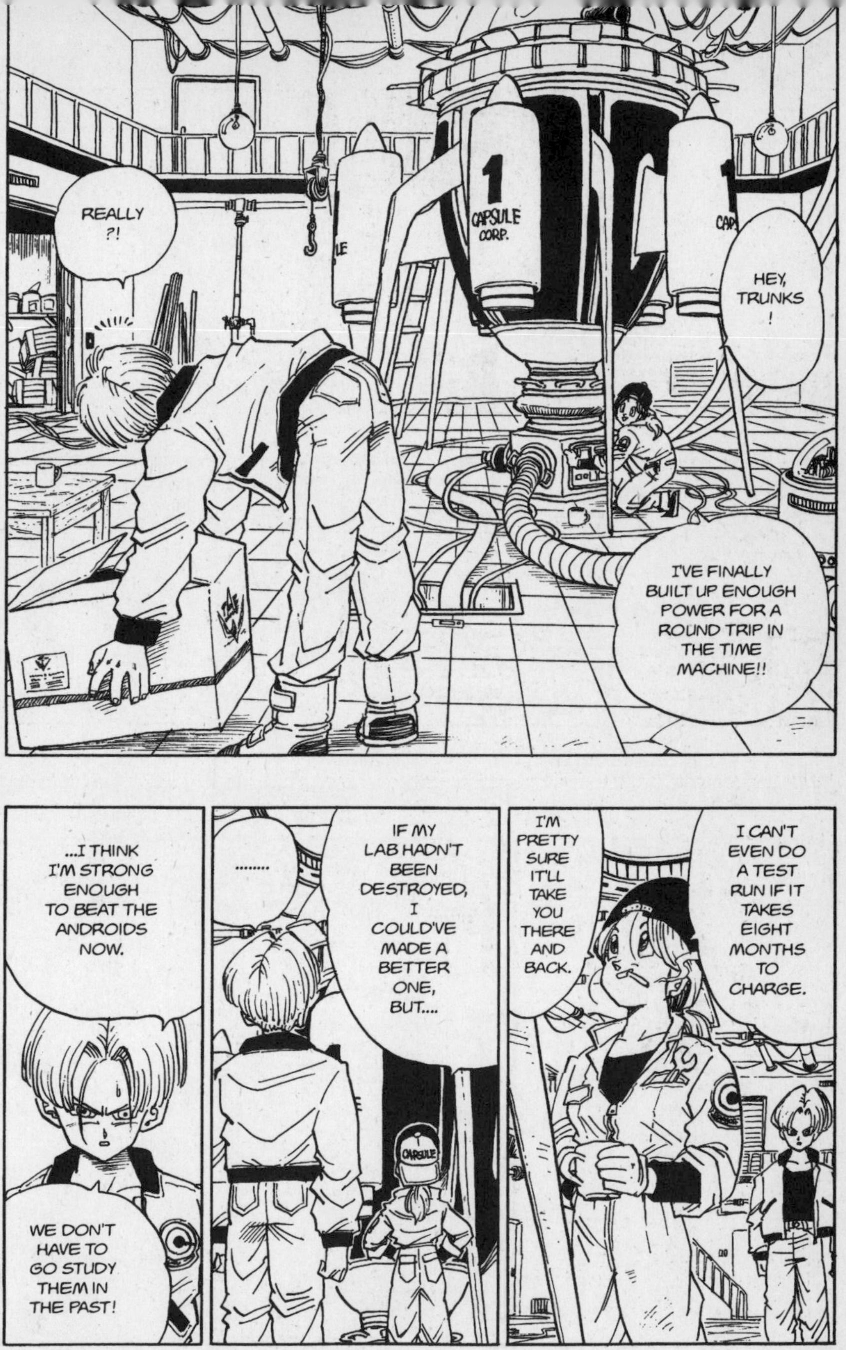

HEY, TRUNKS!
I'VE FINALLY BUILT UP ENOUGH POWER FOR A ROUND TRIP IN THE TIME MACHINE!!
REALLY?!
CAPSULE CORP.
I CAN'T EVEN DO A TEST RUN IF IT TAKES EIGHT MONTHS TO CHARGE.
I'M PRETTY SURE IT'LL TAKE YOU THERE AND BACK.
IF MY LAB HADN'T BEEN DESTROYED, I COULD'VE MADE A BETTER ONE, BUT....
....
...I THINK I'M STRONG ENOUGH TO BEAT THE ANDROIDS NOW.
WE DON'T HAVE TO GO STUDY THEM IN THE PAST!

READ THIS WAY

IT'S NOT THAT SIMPLE. SURE, YOU'RE STRONG. BUT HAVE YOU FORGOTTEN THAT THEY KILLED GOHAN THREE YEARS AGO?
DO YOU REALLY THINK YOU'RE ANY STRONGER THAN HE WAS THEN?

I CAN BEAT THEM NOW, MOM! I KNOW I CAN!
WE INTERRUPT THIS BROADCAST FOR A REPORT ON THE ANDROIDS.
THEY ARE NOW ATTACKING 300KM SOUTH OF WEST CITY...

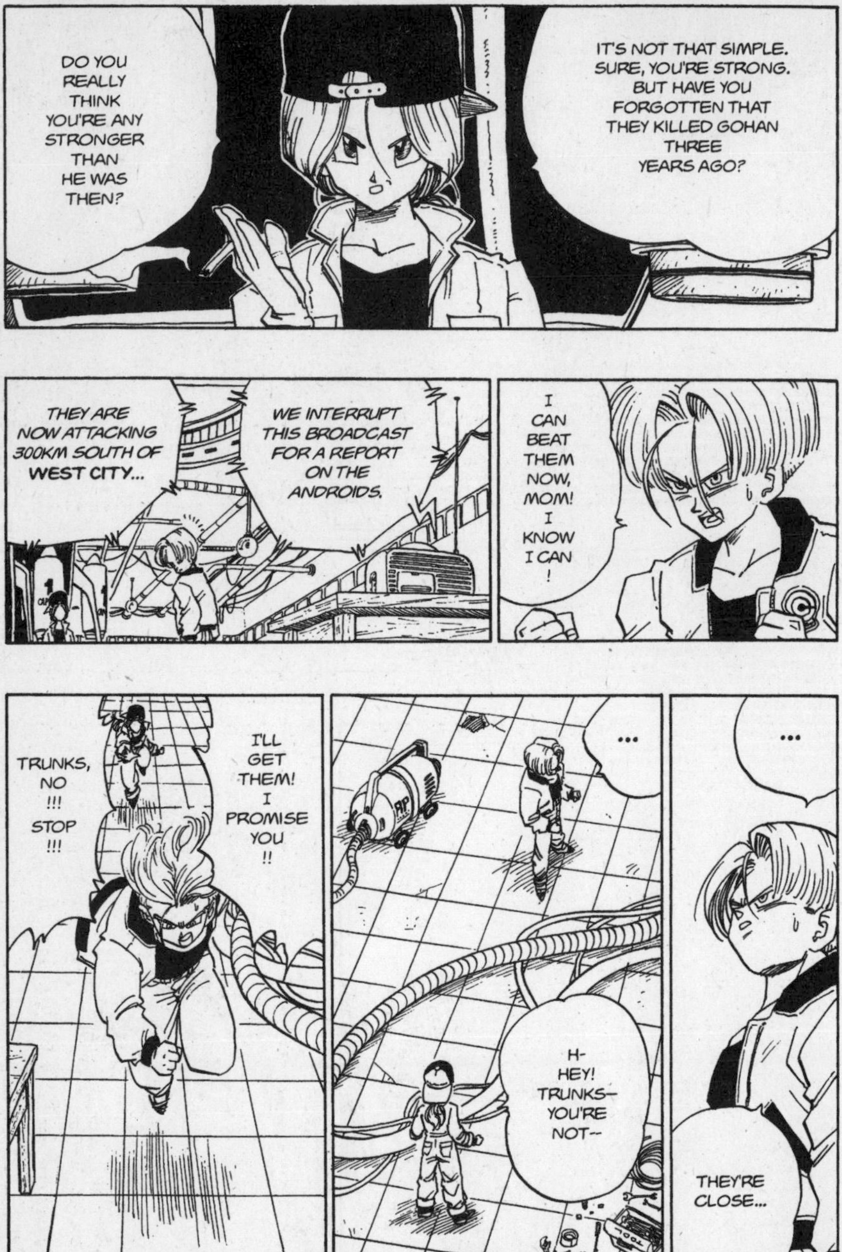

...
THEY'RE CLOSE...
...
H-HEY! TRUNKS— YOU'RE NOT--
I'LL GET THEM! I PROMISE YOU!!
TRUNKS, NO!!! STOP!!!

BM

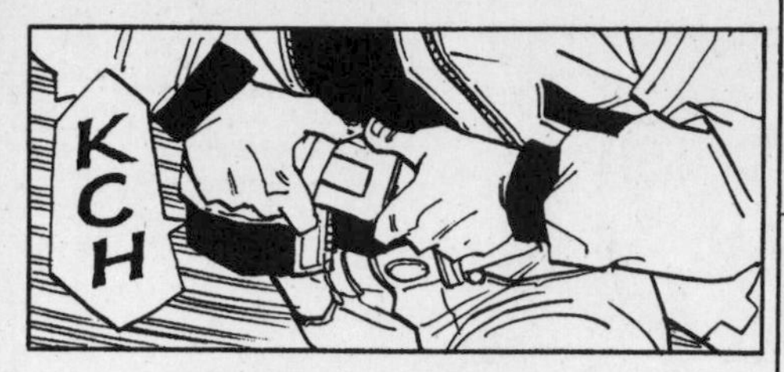
KCH

I'LL AVENGE **ALL** THEIR DEATHS TODAY!!
JUST **WATCH** ME !!!

BOOM

READ
THIS
WAY

FIVE DAYS LATER, IN A SMALL HOSPITAL IN THE WESTERN CITY SUBURBS...

MOM...
YES?

YOU WERE RIGHT... THE ANDROIDS WERE STILL MORE POWERFUL...
I DON'T KNOW HOW I MADE IT HOME ALIVE...

YOU'RE LUCKY, THAT'S HOW. JUST LIKE ME.

FIRST YOU'LL GO 17 YEARS BACK, AND GIVE GOHAN'S DAD HIS MEDICINE. EVERYTHING STARTS THERE.

I DON'T THINK THE WORLD WOULD'VE TURNED OUT THIS WAY IF HE HADN'T DIED...

I'LL GIVE THE TIME MACHINE A TRY AS SOON AS I GET BETTER.

WAS HE THAT POWERFUL?

YEAH, HE WAS... BUT THAT'S NOT ALL.

HE WAS THE KIND OF GUY WHO MADE YOU BELIEVE THAT HE COULD MAKE THINGS RIGHT, NO MATTER HOW TERRIBLE THE SITUATION SEEMED...

READ THIS WAY

I CAN'T WAIT TO SEE MY DAD.

......

...DON'T GET YOUR HOPES UP TOO HIGH.

HERE'S THE MEDICINE.

OK. YOU BE CAREFUL, MOM.

I'M COUNTING ON YOU!

I'LL BE BACK SOON !!

TRUNKS THE STORY: THE END

TITLE PAGE GALLERY

DRAGON BALL
DBZ:194 • Cell's Idea
鳥山明
BIRD STUDIO
FEAR ME, WARRIORS! I AM THE STRONGEST!
ドラゴンボール

These title pages were used when these chapters of **Dragon Ball Z** were originally published in Japan in 1992 in **Weekly Shonen Jump** magazine.

DRAGON BALL
ドラゴンボール
とりやまあきら
鳥山明
BIRD STUDIO
DBZ:196
The Emergence
TIME TO TRAIN...
OR TIME TO DIE!

DRAGON BALL
とり やま あきら
鳥山明
BIRD STUDIO
DBZ:197
The Calm Before the Storm
LET'S TAKE A BREATHER BEFORE THE FIGHT.
ドラゴンボール

DRAGON BALL ドラゴンボール

DBZ:198

Cell vs. the Army

とりやまあきら 鳥山明 BIRD STUDIO

WHAT'S YOUR PLAN, GOKU!? WHY AREN'T YOU WORRIED?

DRAGON BALL
ドラゴンボール
DBZ:200
The Cell Game Begins!
とりやまあきら
鳥山明
BIRD STUDIO
I'M WAITING, SON GOKU!

DRAGON BALL

ドラゴンボール

とりやまあきら

鳥山明

BIRD STUDIO

DBZ:201 • Heroes Assemble!

HERCULE
I'LL SAVE PLANET EARTH!
CHAMPION

DRAGON BALL

ドラゴンボール

とりやまあきら
鳥山明
BIRD STUDIO

DBZ:202

Hercule, Champion of the World

LET THE GAMES BEGIN!

IN THE NEXT VOLUME...

The day of the Cell Game has come—the day when Earth's champions must compete to save the entire human race from destruction. All along, Cell has longed for a match with Goku, to crush the world's mightiest hero and establish its supremacy over all creation. Both of them have enough power flowing through their bodies to destroy the earth. But Goku knows something that Cell doesn't...

AVAILABLE NOW!

HSSS---

SHONEN JUMP
NARUTO
SHONEN JUMP
THE WORLD'S MOST POPULAR MANGA
On sale at WWW.NARUTO.COM
Also available at your local bookstore and comic store.

RATED
T
FOR TEEN
ratings.viz.com

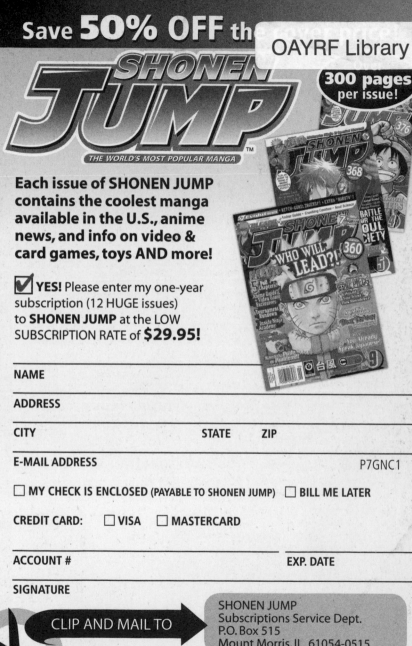